WORKING TOWARD HARMONY

A Memoir

MY JAPANESE GRANDFATHER'S WORDS OF UNDERSTANDING FOR FINDING MY WAY IN THE USA

"I truly loved the book! It was interesting from not only a historical perspective, but culturally, inspirationally, and personally. The logical progression of the book, plus the use of your own voice and insights made the book quite compelling. The actual storyline and your vivid recollections significantly enhance the text. At times, I felt your descriptions to be lyrical. Your readers will connect with your amazing spirit through your writing and feel as though they know you personally as a friend." Peggy Kubitz

Hide Yamatani, Ph.D., MSW, MBA

Published by Hide Yamatani, Ph.D., MSW, MBA

Print ISBN: 979-8-218-03212-8

REVIEWERS' COMMENTS

"I found your story heartwarming, uplifting, and fascinating, both in recounting one person's cultural journey and in describing an American society as generally receptive to welcoming an immigrant whose ethnicity differed from what commonly prevailed at the time. In today's present environment of turmoil and strife, hearing tales of kindness is a tonic for the soul." TOM LEGGE

"First of all, let me say, I truly loved the book! … It was interesting from not only a historical perspective, but culturally, inspirationally, and personally. …the logical progression of the book, plus the use of your own voice and insights made the book quite compelling. The actual story line and your vivid recollection and insights made the text significantly enhanced. At times, I felt your descriptions to be lyrical. Your readers will connect with your amazing spirit through your writing and feel as though they know you personally as a friend." **PEGGY KUBITZ**

"Your story is fascinating and left me thinking about many things even after I put it away. … I feel as if I could take another few hours to chat with you about this book, I really love it so much. My favorite part was hearing the differences between growing up in Japan versus the US. The personal differences show your grandfather's point that people are people, no matter which borders they live between." **NATALIA TOWER**

"Thank you for sharing your fascinating memoir. I found it to be engaging and beautifully written. If this tells you anything, I read the entire book in one sitting. It brought tears, laughter and sometimes even anger. This book is a testament to a life not without challenges, but certainly a life well lived." **JUDY WESNER LATTA**

ACKNOWLEDGEMENTS

Since the beginning of this writing venture, the quality of my life has been enriched by three key individuals- Dr. Solveig Spjeldnes, Kevin Peters, and Alexandra Jaffe. I am deeply indebted to their generous offerings of creative suggestions, kind thoughts and vast array of instrumental assistance that were driven by unwavering compassion and understanding.

AUTHOR'S OVERVIEW

This memoir focuses on the impact of the life lessons my grandfather taught me in post WWII Japan. After my father wrote an editorial against federal land reform policy, my parents were forced to divorce. Believing that, as a Catholic and divorced mother in Japan, she had no future, she married a GI from Pittsburgh and left Japan without us- me (age 3) and my younger brother (age 2). My grandfather raised us to find serenity using his self-written guide, Words of Understanding. As we reached teen years, our mother finally sent for us to live with her in the US. We knew no English and nothing about American culture. We learned to live in the suburbs of Pittsburgh with our estranged mother and a stepfather we didn't know.

Due to the historical accounts of the US-Japan relationships and how fellow US citizens and their public leaders treated

Japanese Americans, my grandfather was deeply concerned about the cultural and social difficulties we could face in the US. He suffered a serious stroke just three days before our departure to the US.

In contrast to my grandfather's worries, most people I met were overwhelmingly caring, supportive, and dignified from my earliest days in the US. If my grandfather had witnessed their goodness and kind hearts, I believe he would have described my all-white Eastwood friends and teachers, as a collection of walking saints and angels.

The reason why so many people treated me with goodwill resulted from my practicing my grandfather's Words of Understanding. In essence its nurturing spirit was being reflected-back to me. Therefore, I am immensely grateful to my grandfather for guiding me through his words and deeds onto the right pathways throughout my life. The honorable, dignified, and virtuous blessings he bestowed upon us were his keynote to Heaven.

Chapter 1

MEETING OUR MOTHER IN THE USA

In March of 1961, my mother finally wrote the letter to her father I'd secretly hoped for since she left Japan when I was 3 years old. It was an invitation for my younger brother, Masae (Mas), and me, Hideyuki (Hide) to live with her in America. She wrote that she and her American husband, our stepfather to be, would meet us in San Francisco in July on nearly the same day as my 14th birthday—just four months away. I was so excited. I had not seen her since she moved to the US with an American G.I., which was 10 years ago or seemed like a lifetime to me and my brother Mas. With Aunt Seiko's help, I had been writing to my mother just about every month, begging her to come back home to Japan. Her letters never indicated that she would be returning to Japan.

I jumped for joy and skipped around the room. Although rarely done, I ran and hugged my grandmother (Sakeko) and grandfather (Suekich) many times, shouting repeatedly "Kamisama, Arigato!" (God, thank you!).

Watching my excitement, my grandfather remained silent. Although he was smiling, he seemed uneasy. He had hoped that my mother, Toshina, (Tosh) would come home to Japan. He had not anticipated that his young grandchildren would leave and follow their mother so far away.

1960 photo of us with grandparents

The letter explained that we would board a cargo-ship from Yokohama—the largest seaport in Japan at that time—that allowed a limited number of traveling passengers. It provided all-inclusive meals with bunk beds and a shared bathroom. Mother wrote that my brother and I would each only be allowed to carry one regular and one small size suitcase on the journey.

Mas's reluctance

Although I was elated about moving to the US, my younger brother Mas was not at all excited about leaving Japan. Mas was a very popular boy in his class with the stature of an adored group leader. Just about every major social event included Mas's presence with his distinguishable social persona. People loved hearing his jokes and stories that he readily shared with his friends. He was definitely viewed as cool and smart by his fellow students and even by older kids.

Mas also stood out because of his unique behaviors, such as climbing up on a tall tree and loudly singing his favorite songs for everyone to hear. This embarrassed my grandmother who quickly demanded he descend from the tree. He entertained kids with card tricks and magic that impressed even my grandfather. Mas was admired also because of his candor and openness. He was confident and comfortable giving impromptu opinions in front of students and teachers. In stark contrast, I was a depressed and angry kid who preferred being left alone. I felt that for no good reason (certainly not due to my fault) we were completely denied our parents' smiles, hugs, and loving words. I had only one friend—Nakasima San—who rarely visited our home but invited me to his home to watch TV. This was a treat because few households had a black and white TV, color was not available yet. I rarely thought about making and nurturing friendships.

Mas was also reluctant to live in the US because of his doubts about the sincerity of my mother's claims that she missed both of us. During his early childhood, she had agreed to give him up to be raised by my divorced father but he ended up in an orphanage accompanied with her inaction due to the divorce agreement and the risk of possible subsequent bonding, which made the separation even more difficult. However, he rightfully resented what happened and was now even angrier because our mother acted as though nothing bad had happened to him. He felt that her destructive neglect of him was unforgivable. Why would he want to move to the U.S. to live with his estranged mother when he knew that our grandparents and Aunt Seiko adored him as a good child with a promising future of building a loving family of his own? He felt their adulation and sincere love combined with his happiness as an invaluable family member. Thus, for him, there was no good reason to move to the US.

Preparing to leave

When Aunt Seiko learned about our upcoming move, she immediately came for a visit to help us apply for passports, purchase suitcases, books, new sets of pants and dress-shirts, pajamas (which we had never worn before), and large towels. My only concern was how all those things would fit into our suitcases. She also promised that she and her husband, Mituki, would accompany us to Yokohama's seaport, which was about 660 miles away and would take about 15 hours of travel time by train.

During the four months between receiving the letter and leaving for the U.S., time seemed both endless and short. My mother had instructed us to buy a Japanese-English dictionary to begin studying how to say basic words like "thank you," "please," "help," "my name is," "I am going to San Francisco," "where is," etc. She also told us to find books about living in the US and to study and prepare for our new life.

We both maintained our school schedule but it was difficult for me to concentrate on my studies. My mind kept getting distracted by visions of hugging my mother and telling her how much I missed her. By the beginning of the last month before our departure date, we withdrew from the school and spent most of our time studying English at home.

My grandfather was worried that we could not speak English and didn't know how to survive in a foreign country. Of course, he understood that my mother would help my brother and me assimilate into the culture of the US, but he also knew that Japanese people were not always treated well there. So, he made sure that we were made aware of the major differences between Japanese and US cultures. As a "student of history," my grandfather was familiar with the Japanese-American internment camps, and the U.S. Immigration Act of 1924 that imposed severe restrictions effectively ending Japanese immigration to the U.S. Finally in 1952, the

US enacted the McCarran-Walter Act that allowed Japanese immigrants to become naturalized US citizens. I'm certain that my grandfather worried that we would face discrimination and worse. Thus, in addition to teaching me about life, he also quickly taught me about the history of Japan and US relations.

As soon as I had turned 13 in July 1960, my grandfather sat me down and told me that if anything happened to him, I would become the head of the household. Following Japanese tradition, he was preparing me to take charge of running the household and the farm. I would be responsible for my grandmother and younger brother Mas's welfare. And as one of the few Catholic families in Japan, he also wanted me to make sure the family stayed deeply engaged with the church affairs and activities.

As part of my training, my grandfather had prepared his own small notebook titled, "Words of Understanding." He had painstakingly written many pages filled with life lessons that he used to teach and discuss with me. He did explain that some of these statements may not apply to me immediately but would be important for my future survival and life of understanding. So, during the preparation period, my grandfather continued to teach me life lessons from his notebook.

He also kept saying how much he and my grandmother would miss us, and he hoped that we would come back and visit them as soon as we could. As we got closer to the final departure date, I saw his silent tears during our family dinners. He ate quietly and kept looking at us in silence as though he wanted to clearly record the visions of our presence in his mind. It was also noticeable that he began losing his appetite and often refused his favorite desserts. Although I was still very excited about finally meeting my mother, I started to feel sadness—a hollow feeling in my chest and confusion as to what to say to him and my grandmother. All I could think to say was, "Thank you for everything" ("arigato gosaimasita"), and that I would always remember their kindness and caring for my younger brother and I. Furthermore, that I had learned so much from his knowledge and wisdom.

As time got closer to our departure date, he was feeling increasingly ill. He started to take long naps and forget to shave or change his clothes. He started refusing to attend the neighbors' get-togethers. I think he felt that it was bad enough that our future life may be filled with strife but even worse, he would be unable to care for and protect Mas and me.

Grandfather suffering stroke

Three days before our departure date, my grandfather suffered a serious stroke, was treated by a doctor at home and became bedridden.

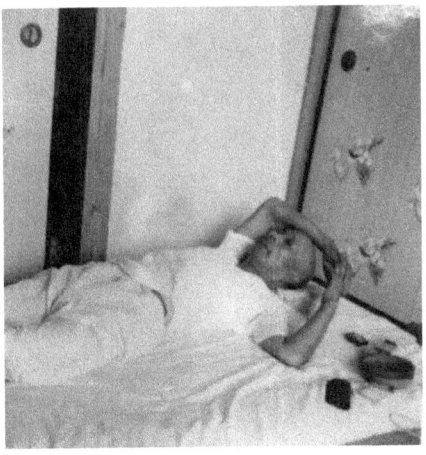

Grandfather with stroke

He could not walk or talk well but,

with assistance, he was able to swallow his specially prepared soft meals. He understood what we said to him and wanted a small portable Sony radio beside him to listen to the news and talk shows. Due to the heat during the month of July, he did not want sheets on him as he laid in his futon bed until late evening hours. He accepted no medicine.

I spent my last few nights unable to sleep, awake with anxiety over the coming trip and the sadness of leaving my grandfather alone. There was no special dinner or gifts given to us, just days dominated by mostly silence between all of us. Only a few basic questions and "yes" and "no" answers were exchanged between us: "Do you have your passport safely in your main suitcase?" Where are you keeping the tickets for the ship?" Is your Japanese-English dictionary already packed?" and "We have to leave by one PM to walk down to the bus station."

The day of our departure, nearing one PM, my initial excitement started to dissipate and I began to feel drained and panicked. My grandfather signaled both of us to come near his bed. The words he uttered to us were "domo sumimasen" (I am sorry). He was sorry for suffering a stroke and being unable to accompany us to Yokohama and see us depart to the US.

Hearing his last words, I was overcome with feelings of guilt, remorse, and shame for not having the guts to postpone our trip to the US and stay until he is better. I looked away, blinking back tears in my eyes. I thought to myself that I was a selfish person that didn't care about my grandfather, who gave his best to raise us and look after our needs. He was the only devoted father figure I ever had, and I loved and deeply admired him.

Leaving Our Home in Japan

As we started to walk to the bus station, which was only about a mile away from our house, I felt the heaviness of my large suitcase. Mituki and Seiko both took our smaller suitcase so we could manage other ones. The bus was slightly late but nearly empty. My grandmother was in tears saying, "Remember to let us know right away when you get together with your mother. Don't forget we love you and you can come back anytime. And tell your mother that we wish the best and pray for all of you every day."

We both hugged her for last time with tears pouring down our cheeks and I said "Domo arigato gosaimus" (Thank you for everything). We promised that we would write to let them know how things went during our trip.

We took the seats near the front of the bus and within 30 minutes or so we were dropped off in the front of the Kokura train station. Mituki already knew where to go to board the train, so we simply followed him. Unlike the bus ride, the train station was busy with an enormous amount of people. Luckily our train was not at all packed like the others, and we were able to drop off our suitcases near our seats and sit down next to a large window. The views on the way to Yokohama were spectacular with dramatically vertical mountains so close to the train tracks. We passed by large, flat, and water filled rice patties, lakes with lots of pine trees hanging over, and rivers with fast moving water.

But the train ride to Yokohama seemed much longer than 15 hours. Several hours into the train ride, I started to feel sick thinking about how the trip would go. I started imagining the worst-case scenario, asking myself panicked questions like: What if my mother is nowhere to be found in San

Francisco? They could get delayed due to an auto accident, take the wrong highway and get lost, or their car could break down. We had only so little money to eat or stay overnight at a hotel. What if I get sick and can't take care of Mas—or myself? I'd never been on a ship for more than a few hours, and I had gotten seasick every time. What if the ship hits severe weather—what would we do? There's no way we'd be lucky enough to have a sunny and calm sea for the entire 11 days on the Pacific Ocean, especially during the month of July.

What if we disliked—or even hated—our new American stepfather? It seemed to me to be possible that he wouldn't grow to love us like our grandfather did. All those worries were not only related to the unknown tomorrow, but they were made worse by the fact that we could not speak or understand English well enough to effectively manage our affairs and the challenges we could potentially face. This worrying kept me up all through the train ride.

I watched trees speed by the train as I ticked through these questions in my mind. I suddenly realized that I might never see my home country, Japan, again, and that I would definitely miss it. I cautiously looked at Mas and thought that he is likely to miss Japan even more than I. He may become a forever-changed person growing up with difficulties and struggles in the USA. I worried that he might even feel how I felt the last few years, sad and angry.

In contrast, Seiko and Mituki seemed to have no problem falling asleep on their hard seats with thin cushions. Occasionally they got up to purchase meals from the train's window at the stops or to visit the bathroom. But my brother and I could not eat much—we only consumed ramune, a ginger ale-like soft drink, with a few bites of seaweed-covered rice balls. Later, Seiko bought us some cookies hoping we would eat something.

At Yokohama train station, my other aunts, who were both Catholic nuns, came to see us off and bring details of our departure back to our grandparents. They offered encouraging words and prayers and told us that they'd be thinking of us and praying every day at their church until they heard that we connected safely with our mother in San Francisco. They told us we should always remember and thank God that with his help, everything will be okay.

Before our departure, I put on my new school cap. I decided to wear it at least until we got on board the ship because I felt that I needed to look older than 13 and smarter than I really was. After all, I was responsible not just for myself, but also for my younger brother's safety and welfare.

Photo at Yokohama with Mituki, Aunt Seiko, Mas, Me and my two other aunts (Sisters Monica and Leoni)

I was nervous about my brother and I traveling on our own—and my Uncle Mituki added to my anxiety when he demanded that we hand over all the money in our wallets because he said the ship provided free meals. Looking at everyone, they seemed to support his assertion—which to me sounded more like a demand—so we reluctantly pulled out all our bills and handed them over to Mituki.

We had no American dollars either, so I felt like I was now walking the gangway naked with no money to use at all during our 11-day trip on an American ship.

Crossing the Pacific

As my brother and I boarded the ship to America, I started to feel drained and nauseous. There were hardly any other Japanese passengers boarding the ship.

Photo from the ship as we were departing Japan

We had to survive on a ship for a week and a half with a seriously limited knowledge of English and no money. Our initial tasks were overwhelming: we needed to guide ourselves to our bunk room, find the bathrooms, cafeteria, and main security office—in case we got into trouble—on a huge cargo ship with 70 or so other passengers roaming around.

We finally found our small, windowless room (lower third floor, # 47 as noted in our tickets) where we'd be sleeping for the voyage and claimed a set of slim bunk beds. They had several two-tier bunks squeezed into the tiny room with enough space under the lower bed to store our suitcases. Our bunkmates were a mix of three Americans and one other Japanese passenger (including the two of us), all older and a bit intimidating.

Luckily, the Japanese passenger, Takahasi San, could speak English. As the ship took off from the Yokohama Bay and as we were settling down in the room, I introduced my brother and myself and asked for his help to figure out where and when meals were served. He warned us that since it was an American cargo ship (not a passenger ship) with mostly American travelers, no Japanese dishes were available. He also noted that the reactions of some Americans at that time were appalling. Japanese sushi, for example, was thought to be a barbaric and germ-infested meal to be avoided.

At our first dinnertime, Takahashi San was nowhere to be found. Luckily, he had already shown us the location of the large cafeteria, which had about 25 tables for 2 and up to 6 diners. A waiter in an all-white Navy like uniform came to us as we were sitting down and handed me a menu. He muttered something about water and so we just nodded as he walked away. Upon his return with water, we had to order from a list of unfamiliar dishes, all in English with no pictures of the dishes (unlike many restaurants' menus in Japan). Looking around, no one seemed to be open to helping us choose what to order. I saw one Japanese lady but she was seated with several others too far away from our table. After a few moments he walked away, apparently saying he'd be back.

I tried using our dictionary to look up words on the menu but that was unhelpful— none of the definitions seemed to describe the dish fully. For example, stuffed cabbage had to be looked up as two separate words. While I understood the individual meanings of "stuffed" and "cabbage," my Japanese-

English dictionary did not have those two words together.

So I guessed, and we ordered four different items—two different items each for my brother and I—in the hope that we would like at least one of them. Sure enough, one of the dishes—stuffed cabbage—was so good. I had never tasted anything remotely close to stuffed cabbage before, but it had some rice mixed with other ingredients inside that tasted wonderful. We remembered to order it continually during our subsequent dinners.

Ordering breakfast and lunch was much easier. I knew English words like egg or egg sandwich and orange juice. A few of the Japanese passengers eventually found out that we needed help with English, so they came around to our table and advised us as to the oishi (delicious) dishes. Subsequently, I felt much better and looked forward to our mealtime to see their friendly smiles and converse in Japanese.

During the evenings I prayed in silence as I laid on the bunk bed just before falling asleep. I reminisced about how my grandfather had taught me that "God is not there to give you things, only to help you work harder for the right missions and to help you focus your efforts. So, you should never pray to God asking for something, only to ask for the strength to continue to do the right things."

He emphasized that my prayer should:

First, thank God for several good things in your life like being healthy, having a loving family, good friends, or other worthy things that come to your mind.

Second, pray for good wishes to other important people in your life like for your Aunt Seiko to be happy with her new husband through an arranged marriage and their new home.

Finally, ask for God's blessing on your effort or commitment to earn what you are wishing for. For example, instead of outright praying for your new Sony radio you want as a Christmas gift, request for his blessing as you save and earn extra money to be able to buy the radio yourself. Or instead of asking for an A on your next math test, pray that you will do your best to study long and hard but you would like his blessing on gaining confidence when taking the exam.

I always hugged a card that my Aunt Seiko had given me for the trip; a picture of a Japanese looking Mary dressed in a kimono with the baby Jesus. So, I thanked God for the good things that came to my mind first, good wishes to my grandfather, grandmother, my aunts, that we continue to be good passengers, help us receive kindness from other passengers, and then finally prayed that we stay focused on positive thoughts and safe blessings during our trip to San Francisco.

My card of Mary and baby Jesus

After a few days on the ship, Mas and I got used to the swaying ship. The best remedy for oncoming seasickness, we discovered, was to immediately go to the bunk bed and lay down until we felt better. This strategy worked incredibly well, so we were virtually free of the seasickness during subsequent travel days.

The Pacific Ocean was so many shades of crystal blue, and I had never seen anything like it. During the day its salt water seemed to light up in fluorescent color. The waves were amazingly clear, and I spent hours staring over the side of the ship, looking deep into the ocean where many large fish and occasionally blue sharks swam—all exceptionally colorful, graceful, and fast.

Views of the sunrise and sunset over the ocean were so exquisite that nothing since seems to compare to their alluring beauty and magnificence. Staring at the beautiful scenery made me feel tranquil and more comfortable about our journey. I had the sudden sense that my aunts' prayers were really working and helping us to feel more secure and blessed. A realization of such thoughts began to make me feel even more excited about finally reuniting with my mother. I also began to feel confident about learning to live with her, even in a foreign land where we would be struggling to adjust while learning a new language and customs. Still one of my biggest concerns was how we would get along with our new American stepfather. Because we grew up parentless, I had no clear idea how to relate to a foreign-born stepfather.

Our first stop was Honolulu Hawaii which featured stunning mountains and beautiful beaches surrounding the island. As the ship approached the large port, we were told to line up on the top deck with our passports and declare if we were bringing anything with us to the US. One of the ship's officers handed us a sheet to declare our items, but we needed help because I couldn't read the sheet which was written in English. I quickly looked for Takahashi san but he was nowhere in sight.

Meanwhile, my younger brother was sick and told me he had to go to the bathroom immediately. I panicked. Where we had to line up had no indications of any nearby bathroom. And if we were to go back to our public bathroom, we not only disobeyed the line-up rules but also could miss filing our papers and stamping our passports. But we had no choice; my brother would have had an accident for sure if he had tried to hold it. So we rushed down three decks, and I waited until he was done then rushed back up to the main deck. Luckily, we were the last two people in line to file our papers and get our passports stamped. The American officer was very kind. He smiled and waved his hand to get to the station. Then, still smiling, he took our passports, stamped them and guided us to simply sign the sheets. We had nothing to declare.

As the ship stopped and its gate lowered to the port's walkway, several Hawaiian women boarded and handed us welcome leis—necklaces strung with beautiful flowers. Takahashi San let us know that the captain had announced that the ship will unload various cargoes at the port and this task will take about 8 hours.

With passport in hand passengers were permitted to look around Hawaii, as long as we were back within 6 hours. Takahashi San guided us to exit the ship, but I told him that we had no money, that my uncle took it because this ship was all-inclusive. He wondered how anyone could travel this distance and not have any money. He could not believe it. "Ok, so just in case, you two should stay close to the ship, but Hawaii is a beautiful place—don't miss it."

Even though no one greeted us, I felt like we were welcomed into a beautiful new country with a magnificent blue sky looking down on gorgeous mountains, surrounded by strikingly elegant beaches. The pleasant ocean breeze cuddled us with reassuring affection, and I felt safe and secure even though I didn't know how to read or speak the language. Curiously, we walked around the port, entered nearby stores, and sat in a small park with several bench seats watching people as they passed by us. Hawaiians looked so healthy and taller than a typical Japanese person. And the young women were so exotically beautiful looking, many must be biracial or multi-racial, such combinations of people were simply not seen in the homogeneous country of Japan.

Photo of Takahashi San with us arriving in Hawaii

Arriving in San Francisco

On the morning of July 24, 1961—the 11th day of our trip—the ship's captain loudly announced that we would be crossing under the Golden Gate Bridge in about 30 minutes, immediately before the port of San Francisco. Just about every passenger gathered on the deck to view the beautifully designed, massive bridge. As we passed under it I could see so many shiny cars and huge trucks as well. I also noticed that, unlike in Japan, I did not see any motorcycles crossing the bridge. But looking at San Francisco Bay and its beautiful surrounding landscape, I felt a surge of wellness and privileged feelings of finally being able to reunite with my dear mother, whom I had dearly missed.

I said to Mas, "We made it, Mar Chan!" I thanked him for being so good throughout the journey and told him that I thought our aunts' prayers must've helped us. But he seemed nervous and unhappy. Looking at his sad face, I realized that he was still concerned about the prospect of meeting unfamiliar strangers—our estranged mother and new American stepfather.

As we walked down the gangplank off the ship, we were guided through the U.S. Customs security station. Fortunately, Yamada San was with us. He kindly directed us through the security check and even inquired for us as to where the waiting guests would be stationed to meet the passengers.

As we approached the meeting station, I heard my mother's voice, "Hide Chan, Mar Chan, koko ne" (right here!). I immediately felt tears spring to my eyes as we approached them. My mother looked exactly like the pictures my grandfather kept of her at home. And my first impression of my American stepfather was how tall he was—at least a foot taller than my mother.

We hugged and cried together, repeatedly

saying, "Yokatta ne" (so good!). Then my mother held me and looked at my eyes and said, "Happy birthday Hide Chan—you will be 14 tomorrow. And you will be fine from now on." I was somewhat perplexed with her words because I immediately thought about my grandfather and told her how well he took care of us, that he suffered a stroke just several days before our departure. She again began to cry and told our stepfather about my grandfather, whom he had met several times in Japan. According to my mother's translation, my stepfather told us in English, "I am sorry, and hope he will recover soon." I also requested that we send our cards as soon as possible to everyone, especially to our grandfather, letting them know that we arrived OK and we were driving to our new home in Pittsburgh. My brother Mas remained reserved but my mother kept hugging him as though he needed to be woken up.

As we walked to the parking lot, she spoke to us in Japanese, asking if we were hungry and what we liked to eat. By then we knew that no Japanese food would be available for us in the US. We ended up stopping for hotdogs and a new soft drink we never had tasted before in Japan: root beer. We both liked root beer so much that every stop we kept shouting, "Root beer!"

The day after we left San Francisco, we woke up in a motel near the highway I-80 in Nevada. My mother again hugged me and said in English, "Happy Birthday, Hide Chan!" My stepfather immediately noted that there are no diners nearby. He seemed to be in a hurry so we agreed to skip breakfast. We kept driving until near lunchtime and finally stopped to eat at a small family-owned restaurant. My mother requested a cupcake with a candle on top. As the waitress brought the cupcake, my mother and stepfather sang the happy birthday song, which I had heard in Japan watching the American TV show I love Lucy.

The trip from San Francisco to Pittsburgh took 5 days. It was a very long drive, but we made it without any serious incident. The whole trip had very little discussion among us. Apparently, my stepfather had forbidden us from speaking in Japanese to force us to adopt the English language as soon as possible. But our mother did not make it clear that our stepfather wanted us to stop speaking in Japanese. She might have felt that at least in the beginning we would need to rely on the Japanese language. We learned later that they disagreed about stopping the use of Japanese starting on day one of our arrival. But we could sense that such was the case as she spoke mostly in English during the drive to Pittsburgh. Still, I didn't blame our stepfather much for such a requirement since he most likely wanted to understand what we were talking about as well. And so our discussion during the long ride remained minimal and basic. My mother would ask, "Are you OK? Hungry? Do you need to go to the bathroom?" The trip would have felt extremely long but due to the new and beautiful scenery of the American landscape, it was bearable. Even Mas was amazed, looking at the vast, flat farmlands, huge lakes, and rocky, wide deserts unfolding past our windows. We'd never seen any of this in Japan.

As we continued to drive home, I often thought of my grandfather's lesson on happiness. He noted that happiness is a decision you make on your own each and every day. A happy person simply appreciates so many things that life offers far more than an unhappy person. And there would always be more things to appreciate than dislike, denigrate, or feel sad about. Thus, in view of our safe travel across the Pacific Ocean, effortlessly connecting with my parents, and being exposed to such beautiful American sceneries, I realized how fortunate I was as a 14 years old youth.

However, I worried because he also said, "No one can make you or force you to be happy, but any horrible person can wreck your happiness. Thus, be very careful about who you associate with, friends, the girl you intend to marry, and the community that you will eventually reside with your family." Although I understood that parents are not chosen, I did ponder what would happen if our new American stepfather was mean, unreasonable, and offensive. That would surely "wreck" our happiness, especially the life of my younger brother Mas who did not want to reside in the US in the first place.

On the fifth day of our trip, we finally reached Pittsburgh and arrived at our new home.

Chapter 2

GRANDFATHER'S VIEW OF JAPAN-US HISTORY

As already mentioned, my grandfather considered himself a "student of history." He was well read and understood the unique relationship between Japan and the US. and what it was like from each country's perspective. Reflecting, I more clearly understood why he was so worried about my brother and me moving to the US. His dear grandchildren uprooted and brought to live in the US was a nightmare for him. I believe that the reason why my grandfather taught me about the history between the two nations is because he thought that I needed to know the Japanese point of view to help understand the WW2 hysteria. Later in my adult life I did fact check and even found additional, specific details related to his historical accounts. He also wanted me to know how Japanese Americans were ill-treated by their fellow citizens, community, and national leaders.

When the Japanese military defeated Russia (Russo-Japanese War,1905), it drew international attention to race as a topic of debate. White superiority was often a discussion topic, since no other racial group had won against Caucasian countries in prior wars. Japan further increased its influence in Korea and annexed the country completely in 1910. Japan also had plans to eventually take over Manchuria, then China, and later French Indochina. Such military conquests caused racially-fueled labeling of Japan as an evil country by Western powers.

During WW1 (1914 to 1919) the Allies were led by mainly three countries, the United Kingdom, France, and the Russian Empire. The US entered the war as an "associated power." The Central Powers consisted of Germany, Austro-Hungary, the Ottoman Empire, and the Kingdom of Bulgaria. All together WWI resulted in a shocking number of casualties—more than 10 million combatants killed, 20 million wounded, 5 million civilians killed, making it the deadliest conflict in world history up to that time.

Although rarely mentioned in the media, Japan was also an "Associated Power" of the Allies. As noted by National Interest (primarily a military journal), the Imperial Navy of Japan played a crucial role in World War I by neutralizing German naval forces in the Pacific, capturing German-controlled territories in China and Oceania, and sending battleships as far afield as the Indian Ocean and the Mediterranean to help control ship movements of military vessels and commercial transports.

According to my grandfather, in return for these contributions to the Allies, Japanese leaders expected a sizable postwar dividend. They especially looked forward to further enhanced mutual respect and equality for Japan from western, predominantly white, nations.

League of Nations - first international conference

Right after WW1, The Paris Peace Conference commenced formal meetings in 1919 and 1920 in order for the victorious Allies to set peace terms for the defeated Central Powers. Dominated by the leaders of Britain, France, the United States, and Italy, it resulted in rearranging the map of Europe and parts of Asia, Africa, and the Pacific Islands. Germany and the other Central Power countries were uninvited.

At this first international conference Japan proposed to adopt a "racial equality clause" to the covenant of the League of Nations as follows:

> The equality of nations being a basic principle of the League of Nations, the High Contracting Parties agree to accord, as soon as possible, to all alien nationals of States members of the League equal and just treatment in every respect, making no distinction, either in law or in fact, on account of their race or nationality.

The racial equality clause was born out of the discrimination and humiliation that the Japanese faced in the West. As might have been expected, when the Japanese made their intentions known about introducing this clause, the most vehement opposition came from the British delegation and Australia. The British Foreign Secretary Lord Arthur Balfour's comment about the clause is cited as follows: "The notion that all men were created equal was an interesting one. . . . You could scarcely say that a man in Central Africa was equal to a European."

US President Woodrow Wilson asked Japan to withdraw their amendment, but the Japanese delegates refused and insisted on a vote. Delegates from Greece, Italy, China, France, and Czechoslovakia spoke in favor of the Japanese amendment to the League Covenant. A vote finally took place and most of the delegates voted for enforcement. However, President Woodrow Wilson declared that "The amendment could not be carried out because there were strong objections to it."

According to my grandfather, Japanese delegates could not believe such a prejudicial response and their indignation to an ethical principle. The military representatives were especially filled with disgust and anger since their naval and ground forces had significantly contributed toward the Allies' victory.

Naval Treaties of International Washington Conference

Then in the 1921-22 International Washington Conference naval treaties proposal forced Japan (by the votes of the Western power majority) to accept an unfavorable fewer battleship ratio (i.e., 5:5:3 for the US, Britain, and Japan, respectively). Then in 1924 the US legislature passed the Japanese Exclusion Act to shut off Japanese immigration into the US. Furthermore, at the 1930 London Naval Conference Western powers again forced Japan to accept the same uneven ratio of heavy naval cruisers.

A major reason for the forced naval treaties was because the British Empire, France, and the US led the international organizations that described Japan's attempt to colonize Southeast Asia as an inhumane, unethical, and intolerant mission.

A key factor behind Japan's attempts to colonize parts of Southeast Asia was because of their limited farmable land. Japan was dependent on importing 60% of food from other countries (i.e., Japan at that time was only 40% food sufficient). Additionally, Japanese islands offered inadequate natural resources—virtually no oil, natural gas, rubber, copper, aluminum ore, zinc and other resources needed to fuel their manufacturing, construction, and utilities industries.

In contrast, however, the British Empire

had invaded and established a military presence in 171 countries around the world since 1870. Similarly, the French had colonized 20 countries as well. Overall, the British and the French colonized more than 95% of the African continent during the colonial period. Thus, these hypocritical historical complaints were considered an affront to the Japanese government's pride, and such racially discriminatory treatment inflamed the militaristic and imperialist sentiments of Japanese ultranationalists and political leaders.

Then, in October 1940, Secretary of the Navy Frank Knox sent for Admiral J.O. Richardson, Commander-in-Chief of the American fleet in the Pacific. Knox advised him that President Franklin D. Roosevelt wanted a wall of American naval vessels stretched across the western Pacific in such a way as to make it impossible for Japan to reach any of its sources of supplies—a blockade of Japan to prevent use of any part of the Pacific Ocean. Japan's take over in Asia had already led to an oil boycott by the United States and Great Britain (1940). This policy of President Roosevelt was only a bluffing threat, but Japanese military and political leaders saw it as a strategic move and potential future nightmare for Japan.

Attack on Pearl Harbor

Consequently, the attack on Pearl Harbor commenced on December 7, 1941. The Japanese navy sank or damaged 188 US aircrafts, eight battleships, three destroyers, three cruisers, and one minelayer. The damage caused to the Japanese navy was 29 aircraft out of 350. Soon afterwards, the US declaration of the war with Japan proceeded. Although there was no prior agreement to the attack, Germany also declared war on the United States, and subsequently their military alliance with Japan was established.

After intense and tormenting consideration, my grandfather decided to refuse to serve in the Imperial Army when the US declared war on Japan. Even with the tumultuous political relationship between the two countries, he felt Japan needed to promote peace with the US, which held a vast array of natural resources and economic power. However, he disliked President Franklin Roosevelt, whom he believed instigated the Japanese attack on Pearl

Harbor with his unwarranted and flagrant assaults on Japanese leaders. Fortunately, he was eventually allowed to stay home to work because he was a large-scale farmer (the country needed to feed its military personnel) and because of his age (he was nearing 40 at the time).

He cautioned me, however, that wars are decisions of governments and their political leaders, not between the people of the countries.

Thus, he emphasized that I should always respect people of the opposing nations because they are not our enemy. "They are folks, just like you, me, grandmother, and Aunt Seiko." He was fond of America and so had nice things to say about its people and the social policies that focused on the individual's rights. I gathered that he did not want me to lose all my hope of survival in the US by just focusing on potential liabilities.

Treatment of Japanese American

My grandfather was also concerned about the Japanese American internment policy (endorsed by President Roosevelt in 1942) that forced approximately 110,000 Japanese Americans to give up their homes and businesses to be committed into internment camps. The Treasury Department seized all Japanese bank accounts and business. According to Colonel Karl Bendetsen (as noted on the Archive of the Colorado Government), children that were as little as 1/16th Japanese-related were placed in internment camps—infants with "one drop of Japanese blood should be locked-up."

Japanese children lining-up to pledge allegiance to the United States
(Dorothea Lange) via Wikimedia Commons

John L. DeWitt, who administered the internment program, repeatedly told newspapers anti-Japanese American campaigns with quotes such as "American citizenship does not necessarily determine loyalty. . . . We must worry about the Japanese all the time until he is wiped off the map. I don't want any of them here. They are a dangerous element." He also spoke to the national radio audience saying, "There is no way to determine their loyalty. . . . It makes no difference whether he is an American citizen, he is still Japanese."

Japanese American US 442nd Battalion

In stark contrast to the media portrayals and actions from politicians, the Japanese American 442nd Battalion ("Go for Broke") fought valiantly during WWII and rescued large US army battalions, saved several cities in France, and liberated Germany's Dachau Concentration Camp, which housed 3,000 Jews.

The 442nd Combat Team became the most highly decorated military unit in the history of the United States Army—9,486

Purple Hearts issued and 21 Medal of Honor recipients. U.S. Army battle reports show the official 442 Battalion casualty rate of 93%, which was 3.1 times higher than the average. US. Military leaders praised the 442nd Combat Team for their exploits:

John J. McCloy, Assistant Secretary of War was quoted as saying, "Whether in France, Italy or elsewhere, I know of no units in the American Army that fought and persevered more gallantly than did those Nisei (second generation Japanese Americans) companies and battalions."

Major General E.M. Almond also commented publicly that "The Nisei troops are among the best in the United States Army and the respect, and the appreciation due honorable, loyal, and courageous soldiers should be theirs rather than the scorn and ridicule they have been receiving from some thoughtless and uninformed citizens and veterans."

". . . I had the honor to command

the men of the 442nd Combat Team. You fought magnificently in the field of battle and wrote brilliant chapters in the military history of our country. . . . They demonstrated conclusively the loyalty and valor of our American citizens of Japanese ancestry in combat." (General Mark W. Clark).

However, the unit's exemplary service did not immediately change the attitudes of the general US population. Veterans were welcomed home with some signs that read, "No Japs Allowed" and "No Japs Wanted." Many veterans were denied service in shops and restaurants. Others had their homes and properties vandalized as the public hatred of Japanese Americans was kept alive among many fellow countrymen. In 1988, the U.S. Congress passed and President Ronald Reagan signed legislation which apologized for the internment on behalf of the U.S. government. The legislation stated that the government's actions were based on, "race prejudice, war hysteria, and a failure of political leadership."

Safe refuge from the Holocaust

Although rarely noted by the US media, my grandfather was familiar with the fact that Japan, during World War II, was regarded as a safe refuge from the Holocaust, despite being a part of the Axis and an ally of Germany. The Japanese diplomat to Lithuania at that time (Chiune Sugihara) gave targeted Jews entry visas to Japan, saving more than 6,000 lives. Most of them ended up in Kobe, Japan until after the war. It is estimated that more than 40,000 descendants of Jewish refugees are alive today because of Sugihara's swift actions. Israel officially declared him to be a hero of the Holocaust and made him a recipient of the Righteous Among the Nations Medal.

Throughout the war, the Japanese government continually rejected requests from the German government to establish anti-Semitic policies. My grandfather believed that Japan's resistance to Germany's policy reflects the impact of Sugihara's just action.

In contrast, even with millions of European Jews displaced from their homes, the United States had a poor track record of offering asylum in the US. The government turned away thousands of Jewish refugees during WWII. Most notoriously, in June 1939, the ocean liner St. Louis and its 937 passengers (almost all Jewish) were turned away from the port of Miami, forcing the ship to return to Europe. According to the Holocaust Encyclopedia and Smithsonian Magazine, more than a quarter of the passengers were subsequently arrested by the Nazis and died in the Holocaust. U.S. Government officials from the State Department to the FBI to President Franklin Roosevelt himself argued that refugees posed a potentially serious threat to national security.

My remorse

I believe that a major factor that contributed to my grandfather's stroke just three days prior to our departure to the USA from Japan was due to his educated awareness of these historical facts. He justifiably was deeply concerned with the potential cultural and social difficulties that he expected we would face in the US. While he understood my excitement to finally reunite with our mother, he also knew that I had no genuine realization of the potentially devastating impact of racial bigotry.

In stark contrast, I was not caring enough about my grandfather, who was a genuinely dignified individual, loving and caring for his grandchildren. I was self-absorbed and only focused on meeting my mother and stepfather and to look intelligent, healthy, and well-dressed. Even though my grandfather's household finances were tight, I kept complaining and whining that I needed more new clothes—especially western styled attire and new sets of shoes. Realizing my repulsive selfishness much too late in my life, I only ask him to accept my sincere remorse without forgiveness. I deserve to repent until my passing for lacking insight and being foolishly vain.

Residing in a homogeneous country like Japan was difficult enough, but the enormous coping efforts needed to deal with prejudice and intolerance was something else entirely. I am sure that after the arrival of the letter from my mother he had countless sleepless nights and distressing periods of worry.

Chapter 3

PRELUDE TO LEAVING US PARENT-LESS

I DO NOT have any memories of my father, Masanori Matuyama. He was forced to divorce my mother when I was about 18 months old and my brother was about two months old. Based on what I did learn from my grandfather and aunt Seiko, who was two years younger than my mother and lived with us until I turned 13, I wish I had the opportunity to meet and spend time with him to learn more about him. Even at the age of 74, I have never met my father since his departure.

Masanori was a Japanese Imperial Navy pilot trained to fly the Mitsubishi A6M, a long-range carrier-based fighter aircraft. His third mission, scheduled to take place near the Philippines, was called back due to weather-related issues that made the attack and re-landing on the carrier too risky.

My Father and his fighter plane (1944)

As it became clear that Japan would lose the war, along with other loyal comrades, he volunteered to be a "Zero Pilot," those tasked with executing a suicide attack. Fortunately, just before his scheduled zero mission, Japan surrendered to the United States, so his life was saved due to the timely overpowering of Japan by the US military and its Allies (i.e., Great Britain, China, and the Soviet Union).

As a college student, my father majored in journalism. His specialization in journalism was reviews of social and political policies and community affairs. He was preparing to work for a newspaper after his graduation. However, near his graduation a Japanese Navy recruiter approached him and offered him a navy carrier pilot training program. He knew such an offer was only made to an elite group of candidates, so he accepted and enrolled.

In contrast to the navy pilot training, which focused on destroying the enemy, he had taken piano lessons since high school and continued through college. He loved classical music (imported records) and gifted my aunt, Seiko, with one of his LP albums, which was recorded in the US by Eugene Ormandy's Philadelphia Orchestra (in the late 1930s). She kept it (Richard Strauss, Symphonia Domestica) and gave it to me to keep when I turned 13 years old. According to Seiko, he also liked to listen to Chopin, Bach, and Beethoven, whose records she often borrowed from him.

However, my grandfather thought that Masanori was too much of an attention-seeking individual. For example, when my father played the grand piano in the church's small auditorium, my grandfather hated the fact that young women would adoringly surround him. To my grandfather my father seemed to relish and encourage such attention. As a father-in-law, he was even more concerned about possible gossip and rumors that may spread (even baselessly) about involvement with another woman.

Because he was college educated, my father seemed to my grandfather to be arrogant and conceited. He felt that, as a cultured and privileged man, his son-in-law should be more humble and self-effacing—respectful of everyone, especially of his daughter as his devoted wife. Instead, he seemed to be seeking admiration from everyone because he was well educated (very few were in those days) and a highly regarded former pilot in the Japanese Imperial Navy. My mother was also uncomfortable about his attention to overly friendly young women. Nevertheless, she was fascinated that he could beautifully play classical piano.

Correspondingly, perhaps, my father's

siblings stood out also as unusually accomplished young adults, especially for early 1940s Japan. His older brother, Haruto, practiced family medicine in Hiroshima. His younger sister, Yuna, was a college student majoring in German. Just prior to her graduation, she was delegated by the Japanese Intelligence Agency as a team member of German interpreters for Japanese officials stationed in Frankfurt Germany during World War II. After the war she chose to stay and resided in Germany for over 50 years until her passing. His youngest sister, Ayako, majored in English and later became a Catholic nun and taught English at several Catholic high schools.

Unfortunate divorce

Despite the strict Catholic mandate against marital termination, my father was compelled to divorce due to my grandfather's assertion and determination given the norms of society at that time. The primary reason was a controversial newspaper editorial he wrote about the national land reform policy to divide the large lands owned by a substantial number of farmers and landholders across the country. The land reform laws were intended to limit the acreage of farms to a size that one household could sustain—unaided by outside labor. The government also forced landlords with large farmlands to sell them to the government at a low price. The government then sold this land, often to the families who had been farming it for the owners of large farms. Prior to World War II, about one-third of the nation's farmers owned most of the farmlands in Japan. About one-quarter of the owners simply rented their land to hired workers, which generated huge revenues for the upper-class landowners.

This federal initiative was a serious threat to my grandfather who operated a large farm growing rice, fruits (watermelon, peaches, grapes), and an assortment of vegetables (lettuce, pumpkins, tomatoes, zucchini, and potatoes) with the assistance of more than 40 hired worker families during the harvest time. Many workers were needed year-round because Japanese farming at that time was considered inefficient (today some may disagree). For example, peaches and grapes were individually wrapped in a bag handmade with newspapers saved by worker families.

Land reform editorial

According to Aunt Seiko and later my mother as well, my father, who at that time was editor of a small newspaper, wrote an editorial in sympathy to large farm owners' predicament. He wrote about what he felt was the injustice of land reform, believing that owner families had legitimately acquired large lands and offered critical help to the families who often did not have the resources or know-how to manage the farmlands on their own. He also wrote about a significant number of loan predators who were taking advantage of families trying to buy farmland, despite knowing they would eventually default.

These essays stirred local government officials who became increasingly concerned that they would be unable to enforce the land reform policies without public controversy and bring considerable embarrassment to high-ranking representatives of the central federal government. Local politicians, government officials, and the police chief met and decided to arrest my father and charge him with, "Aiding enemy communists by inciting unrest and controversy related to the federal policy."

He was taken to a court that consisted only of judges. Japan utilized a three-tiered judicial system without a peer jury. A new quasi-jury system was passed into law in recent years, but still, there are no peer juries—just "lay judges" (saiban-in) working side-by-side with the "professional judges." Subsequently, he was sentenced to one year in jail, which was relatively light given how seriously local officials viewed his infraction. The judges determined my father's jail time based on the severity of the crime (highly speculative for newspaper articles), his motive (only few thought he was a communist sympathizer), the outcome (which was not quantifiable), the impact on Japanese society (which was loosely estimated), his age (28 – young adult), previous criminal record (none), and degree of remorse shown (most arrested Japanese show remorse even when they believe their innocence). Thus, sentencing depended upon the judge's assessment as well as subjective perceptions, which were related not only to the defendant's stature but also his family's reputation and probable public reactions.

In Japan, as is still true today, having a family member sentenced to jail causes severe reputational damage (in stark contrast to today's potential reactions in the USA). This was especially true and intense among the small Catholic community of devout religious followers. Such a conviction caused acute embarrassment, humiliation, shame, and public disgrace. The family was about to cope with dishonor on a monumental scale.

My grandfather was afraid that if he openly protested the land reform policy he would be branded as anti-federal government and seen as a communist-sympathizing Catholic. As a dignitary of the church, he also was concerned that key community members were carefully watching his reaction to his son-in-law's conviction. A negative public reaction from my grandfather would have brought dishonor to the church community and would invite public condemnations of Catholics, especially because he was a deacon of the church. Thus, he believed that he had to act decisively. So, he publicly reprimanded my father and demanded that my mother and father divorce even though that meant a major desecration of Catholic decree ("divorce is a major sin") and disintegration of his daughter's family.

My father was distraught about the

unfairness of his conviction but agreed he had brought dishonor to the family. He was remorseful, too, about my mother, who was worried about her and his children's fate. He talked with sorrow to my mother about his need to divorce her and separate himself from the family. He also worried that after serving the jail sentence he would be unable to find work in the community. Because there were only a few Catholic communities, it would be extremely challenging for an unemployed Catholic who was a head of household to move to another city and find a decent job.

My grandfather had a long talk with my mother and promised her that his grandchildren would always be cared for in their household as long as she needed their help. So, understanding that there were no other salient possibilities, my mother proceeded with the divorce. Still, she worried about her uncertain and likely, bleak future, and the daunting prospect of raising young children as a single mother. My mother also knew well that in those days most men did not marry a divorced woman with children, especially in Catholic communities.

My brother and I were too little to

realize the major events going on around us. However, my little brother as a young child was an indisputable survivor. My father asked as his last wish that he would get custody of his youngest son. My grandfather told my mother that there is no way the oldest son should be taken away from our family but that he also deserved a son, and besides, my father promised that he would not interfere with how I was raised.

My father also agreed that along with his side of the family, he would never get in touch with me nor go to a family court asking for visiting rights. Perhaps both parties felt that possible bonding between my brother Mas and I would invite difficult family relationships and it would be better with an explicit separation. Thus, as noted previously, I have no recollection of ever seeing my father or his side of the family— even up to this point in my life. Apparently, he moved and lived in the city of Fukuoka, which was far from our town, and my grandfather had no reason to travel to his city. Furthermore, most of my father's family members lived in Hiroshima, and in those days, people generally stayed away from the city which was suffering from radiation illnesses and associated problems after the US atomic bombing.

So, my mother agreed to give him up as a family member, which led later to my brother's profound disappointment with our mother for giving him up that he continued to embrace all the way into his adulthood. My mother must have realized also that raising two children by herself would be much more difficult than raising one. Besides, Mas would be with a college educated and well-established, high-profile father. In those days, very few children had such a family background.

For reasons unclear to me (perhaps because my father was sentenced to a year in jail after his court case), Mas ended-up in an orphanage near Fukuoka. Almost a year later, the orphanage contacted my grandfather and informed him that Mas had accidently suffered a serious shoulder injury and that they would not pay for his hospital and recovery bills. Consequently, my grandfather brought him back home for medical care. Apparently, he suffered tears and inflammation in the rotator cuff of his right shoulder and damaged the connected muscles and ligaments.

This led my grandfather to become deeply attached to Mas. Thus, official papers were refiled, and my brother was able to rejoin our family, breaking the prior agreement that he would live with my father. Again, I do not recall these sad events because I was too young to be aware or remember my brother's tragic experience.

Events after the war

After Japan's official surrender to the US on September 2, 1945, about 350,000 U.S. personnel (mainly military officers and soldiers) were stationed throughout Japan, even in small towns, wherever there were railroad stations, seaports, or bus stations nearby. In those days, local business boomed due to American G.I. 's who had military pay to spend, especially for things like going to restaurants, movie theaters, and venues that brought in musical groups and other entertainment. The demand for restaurant workers skyrocketed because of this. Waitresses were happy to serve American G.I. because they tipped, even though tipping is not customary in Japan.

American GIs socializing with Japanese women
https://www.bbc.com/news/magazine-33857059

As a result, more than 40,000 Japanese "war brides" married American soldiers and moved to the US, endangering everything in the future with their former "enemies." War brides risked not only bigotry in Japan but also in the US. Although war casualty data generated by the military tends to be inaccurate, History.com reported that more than 49,000 Americans died fighting the Japanese military. The number of Japanese killed was far more than that. It is understandable that people on both sides continued to harbor animosity for their former enemies after the war ended. Thus, the decision by Japanese women to marry

American G.I.'s was a seriously worrisome one for them and their families. This was true for my mother.

The following description is entirely based on what my mother told me years later about what our family and her life were like when Mas and I were toddlers.

My mother worked in a restaurant near an American Army barracks that was owned by a fellow Catholic family. When the restaurant began allowing patrons to bring in alcohol, the volume of customers and incidents between disorderly patrons increased significantly. Usually, such incidents typically involved the G.I., not Japanese customers. One day, she met a G.I. who was military police (MP) called in to stop fights at her restaurant. He was commissioned at the nearby train station and worked occasionally as a handyman fixing or replacing various items such as light switches, door locks, and broken windows. She described him as a friendly, convivial, and self-confident G.I. who smiled easily. In those days, most G.I.'s, and many locals, carried an English-Japanese dictionary so they could communicate—with some struggle—about basic matters.

Meeting William Kaminsky

One day, as she was serving him lunch, he introduced himself as William Kaminsky. "Call me Bill," he told her, and asked her for her name. She responded that her name was Yamada. Since Japanese people typically go by only their last name, even today, he also asked what her mother called her. "Toshina," or "Tosh" she said. They exchanged small talk (all in broken Japanese and English) about their hometowns, the food they ate, movies they liked, and how they celebrated holidays. He returned to the restaurant the next day and asked her if she would be interested in one day going to a movie with him—in broken Japanese, but with an "endearing accent," my mother later told us. After thinking about it momentarily, she responded that she was not sure if she would be allowed. She explained that she needed to ask her father for his permission ("sumimasen kedo, father approve ka ne?").

My grandfather reluctantly told her he'd think about it. But he ultimately gave her his OK, if and only if Bill came to meet him and picked her up at the house. He also wanted to know what movie they would see and when she would return home. She did not see him; however, for several weeks because he was assigned to another train station to help assist a team working on a derailed cargo train near the Fukuoka station (the main hub for the Kyushu, southern region of Japan). On his next visit to the restaurant, she told him that her father had given her permission to see the movie. In those days, Japanese movie theaters showed mostly American movies, so many of them were in English with Japanese subtitles to draw the G.I.'s and their Japanese female companions into the theaters.

She dated him for about eight months until he was commissioned to go back to the United States. Several weeks before he was scheduled to sail back to the US, he asked her to please wait for him, saying, "I will be back to marry you," and "Please wait for my letter" (domo omachi kudasai). She didn't say yes because his proposal was totally unexpected, and she had a lot to think about. She was excited, confused, joyful, and uncertain about what this would mean for her, but she decided to immediately tell my grandfather that William had asked her to marry him.

He initially had no response, just a face of bewilderment. He told her, "You should not take him seriously—only a few men will keep such a promise, especially from a man from a foreign land." He then asked, "Does he know that you have two children?"

She reluctantly said, "No, he never asked."

"Well then when he finds out, he will change his mind. You wait and see. So, don't even think about it anymore. This will not happen."

Eventually, he gave my mother the OK to marry William, only if he returned and they wed in Japan. As my mother had already anticipated, my grandfather also understood even more seriously that there was almost no way that my mother would be able to remarry and secure family stability with an adequate household income in Japan. She would never be able to be redeemed in the eyes of Catholic parishioners and develop the perception of family integrity amongst community residents. As a single parent, my mother would have faced undesirable future liabilities and hardships while raising two boys alone. She could have even suffered from the indecent men trying to take advantage of a single destitute woman. This realization must have led to his conclusion that there was no other possibility for her future except to take the chance to marry any good man that liked her, even a foreigner.

I gather my grandfather also felt guilty that he forced my father out of the Yamada family and so he was responsible for resolving my mother's fate as the victim of these most serious consequences. A divorced man could much more easily marry another woman compared to a divorced woman with kids. Thus, he told her he would take care of my brother and me until she was ready to return to Japan (if things didn't work out), or until we were old enough to travel to the United States.

William had a job waiting for him at a steel mill in Pittsburgh. But he did not have enough money saved to travel back to Japan and return to the US with my mother. He had to save most of his wages for eight months and sell some of his belongings in order to purchase a diamond wedding ring, a gift for my grandparents, and enough money to finance the trip.

William's return to Japan

Meanwhile, since my mother did not hear from him, she thought he probably had changed his mind. However, one day a letter from him appeared at her restaurant. She rushed it to a G.I. interpreter of the Japanese language. The interpreter told her that in his letter William had written about how much he loved her and said he would travel back to Japan to meet her during the first week of the following month. It would take him 18 days of travel to get there—five days to drive from Pittsburgh to San Francisco, then an overnight before boarding the cargo ship the next day, 11 days to cross the Pacific Ocean, and one final day traveling from Yokohama to Kokura (a major city near her hometown). He also had a list of papers that she needed to secure and prepare, including her health history, official identification papers, and a passport.

When William finally returned, he and my mother met in the restaurant where she still worked. The first question my mother asked was why he hadn't written to her in so long. He told her that the first two letters he had written were returned as "address unknown," so he had written to his commanding officer to ask him to get the right address of the restaurant where she worked. The ordeal took three months. But he had faith in her and trusted her to wait for him. Also, he had been extremely busy, frequently working two shifts (8 a.m. to 4 p.m. and continuing to midnight) and taking his buddy's weekend and holiday shifts at the steel mill to raise enough money to prepare for their marriage.

He did not get down on his knees to ask if she would marry him, which disappointed my mother who had seen some American movies with such a beautiful scene.

Bill and my mother's early year's picture

In those days, two families arranged Japanese marriages after checking each other's background, educational level, and community reputation. Thus, Japanese grooms almost never directly proposed to the brides and asked for her hand in marriage. William's gesture was not so different from what she considered as customary—for example, my father did not propose directly to my mother before their wedding. But she had seen several movies that showed how a man proposed marriage to a woman by kneeling in a humble and hopeful way. So, in essence, she never said, "Yes," to William because there was no such proposal. But the diamond ring was beautiful. She had never seen such a ring, which was slightly big for her finger, but uniquely stunning.

William had contacted the U.S. embassy and consulate personnel and was told that they could not perform marriages in foreign countries, but marriages legally performed and valid abroad are also valid in the United States. He also was told he did not need to have a registrar attend the ceremony or be present at their venue. He could register his marriage at his local registrar's office on a weekday with official marriage papers. William and my mother were pleasantly surprised, and they invited only her immediate family to be present at the wedding. Within three weeks, they were on a ship heading toward San Francisco.

Leaving us parent-less

I was too little to recall getting a picture taken with my mother, grandfather, and my brother just before she left us to live with William in the US. She probably did say goodbye to us with multiple hugs, but I do not recall such a departure event at all; it must have been somber, not dramatic.

Just before my mother's departure to US - with us and grandfather

Subsequently, my aunt Seiko provided crucial comfort to us. Although she worked full-time as a telephone operator, she would occasionally bring us a new toy or our favorite candies or desserts. I remember oishī (super delicious) American style pies, cupcakes, and cookies. She also patiently spent time with us during many evening hours until our bedtime. However, her account is that we often cried, calling our mother and father's names, especially during our bedtime. We did not understand why both our father and mother were nowhere to be found.

Seiko remembered and told me about the episodes when we woke up during the night crying in near silence. She told me that my grandmother often came to our bed and said, "Don't worry—your grandfather and I will always be here." Seiko also remembered that our pillowcases needed to be washed frequently because of the stains from our tears. She also saw that I often hugged my mother's dresses that were left hanging in the closet, crying out, "Doko ni itta, okasan (where did you go, mama)?"

When she checked on us during the night, my younger brother Mas was holding me or had my hand on his chest trying to comfort me to help me to stop crying. Between the two of us, Mas was the stronger, more resilient child. You may be able to tell this too from following photo— I'm the older brother sitting on the chair looking vulnerable. He continually helped me to manage my own emotional turmoil that refused to go away.

Aunt Seiko and us a few years after
my mother's departure

Chapter 4

FAMILY HISTORY AND MEMORABLE EVENTS

A S NOTED, MY grandparents and their daughters were devout Catholics. Their ancestors had converted to Catholicism back in Nagasaki, Japan where the Catholic religion was first introduced in 1549. Catholicism was practiced in my family with high regard and a history of dedicated commitment.

My grandmother and her daughters
who were catholic nuns

Christianity slowly spread to parts of Kyushu (a southern region of Japan) and into Hiroshima and other northern cities. In 1587, however, the powerful warlord Toyotomi Hideyoshi (1537–98), issued an anti-Christian edict, initiating a movement against the religion that intensified further in 1612 following another edict by the newly established Edo shogunate. Subsequently, Japan entered a period of relative international isolation for two-and-a-half centuries, during which Christianity was officially banned.

An uprising of some 30,000 Catholic converts in southern Japan agitated the Tokugawa shogunate. After the uprising the shoguns ruthlessly persecuted Christians. Countless Japanese converts and European missionaries were executed for practicing their Christian faith. Surviving missionaries were driven out of Japan. Consequently, remaining Catholics went underground, hiding their faith and practicing in small churches often built deep in the mountains until the end of World War II.

A hidden church in Nagasaki Region, Japan

Missionaries slowly returned to spread the faith once more in the second half of the 19th century after the country reopened to international trade. Laws regarding Christianity became more relaxed. But it wasn't until 1947, when Japan's postwar Constitution guaranteed freedom of religion, that Catholics and other Christians could openly practice their religion.

A great irony for Catholic families in Japan occurred when the atomic bomb was dropped on Hiroshima (August 6, 1945). This was the city where my father was raised. Many surviving Catholic families in Hiroshima managed to flee to Nagasaki where their extended families resided, only to be bombed again (three days later.) According to the Agency for Cultural Affairs of Japan, roughly 1.5% of the Japanese population was Christian at that time, and untold but huge numbers of Japanese Catholic families were wiped-out by the bombings. Fortunately, none of my father's family members suffered serious injuries.

Understanding more about my grandfather and his family history will be helpful for my story. It begins with the origin of the crest of the Yamada family, which dates to the Kamakura era (1185-1333), during which paulownia leaves were embroidered on clothes that the imperial families would wear which made people recognize it as the symbol of the imperial family. In the age of civil wars, a Paulownia Crest was handed over from the imperial family to exemplary samurai and to their vassals. The Yamada family was a recipient of the dignified symbol over 200 years ago. The family name Yamada is clearly engraved on this tombstone in Japanese which stands at my great-grandparents' grave.

Yamada family's Paulownia Crest
on the family's tombstone

Having a family crest was a big deal in
Japan in those days. Families wore their crests
on formal dress attire (men and women's
kimonos) for holidays and special events,
such as weddings, funerals of famous people,
and government-sponsored celebrations.

My dear grandfather

The guests always served children of such families with respectful regard, and, in some cases, with an excessive adulation to win good favor from the families. Currently,

Japanese government officials also use a slightly different Paulownia Crest during their attendance to important and formal events and celebratory holidays.

My grandfather in part commanded community-wide recognition due to the family's inheritance of the Paulownia Crest. He was also a highly respected deacon of the Catholic Church, and his three daughters were also well-known Catholic nuns in a charity order. He was also known as a "well-educated person" who had attended high school, and he was proud that he graduated fifth in his class of over 100 students in 1918. During those days, young Japanese students mostly attended their school as nationally required up to 9th grade. To advance further (to high school or college) one had to score high enough to pass the entrance examinations.

He aspired to be a teacher of history because he loved to read historical accounts of Japan as well as Western nations including the US and European countries, especially Germany and England. He read extensively about the United States and was knowledgeable about its social and historical accounts of Japanese and Japanese American affairs. However, right after his high school graduation, his father began to experience failing health. He was then expected to manage the family farm and its workers and needed to put his teaching aspirations on hold.

I remember as a young child (9 years old) my grandfather and I would camp out overnight near the main farm gate from late spring to the end of summer to discourage potential thieves from stealing watermelons, pumpkins, and even premature potatoes right out of the ground. As Japan instituted a major federal land reform initiative at the end of WWII, my grandfather was already suffering from high debt because he lost some key workers to the military and the forced production of rice and other farm products with controlled prices to support the war effort. Such altered farm production practices also led to families in the community suffering from a lack of fruits and vegetables for their daily consumption. So, some hungry townspeople turned into thieves who stole crops from farms like my grandfather's.

We would light our tent with an oil lamp and sleep on mini-futons with attached pillows that we laid on top of a thin board. I would sip a Ramune (a ginger ale like

Japanese soft drink), and he would drink from his heated bottle of sake and eat soy-sauce baked rice crackers. Because grandfather had to euthanize our big and fierce dog (an Akita) after it attacked and seriously injured a worker's child, we were alone against the thieves. We had no watchdog to alert us of any potential villains nearing our farm. So any small noise scared me and kept me awake. I continually envisioned the thieves carrying katanas (long samurai swords) and attacking my grandfather, who had only a baseball bat that could easily be overpowered.

On several occasions, he said, "Don't worry 'Hide Chan,' my sensei taught me the kendo (a sword fighting technique). I am an excellent sword fighter," he would insist. OK, I thought, but he had only a baseball bat.

I also recall during our camping episodes how my grandfather took the opportunity to start sharing some of the simple matters that were part of his Words of Understanding which was more formally introduced to me several years later. For example, he said to me, "As you are trying to go to sleep, think of all the simple but good things that happened (like how beautiful the morning sun was, you finished your math homework on time, your bed feels cool, etc.). Tell your mind that all the sad or worrisome things of the day will be on a waiting list to deal with later—just focus on the good as you fall asleep."

My grandfather had no problem falling into a deep sleep with his loud snores that still did not help me feel safe at all. But because he thought the thieves might be his workers or their sons, he felt he should not hurt them. He simply wanted to scare them off by yelling ferociously and acting aggressively. Most thieves during those days covered their faces so, if seen, they could run away, unidentified, into the darkness.

A few years after WWII, due to living under crushingly rigid federal regulations, he, along with many other farmers, was taxed into poverty. My grandmother told me that in response to the forced economic destitution he suffered from serious depression. For several months, my grandfather could not get out of bed on time in the morning to oversee the farms. I was 9 years old at that time.

Eventually, he had to sell his remaining farmland and large house to pay off the debt. He moved the family about 75 miles north to another region called Sone, near the northern city of Kokura, which is in Kiyushu, the most southern major island of Japan. He was able to build a new but much smaller house and operated a few rice pads and fruit tree plots. To supplement the household income, he raised some 20 or so chickens to sell eggs and raised a few pigs for meat packing companies.

Building a new house

I still recall how our small, ranch style three-bedroom house was being built. I was expected to stay away from the building site, but I couldn't help but be near them and watch how they built the house. There was no basement dug under the house. Instead, a deep hole was dug into the ground and filled with cement to stabilize the main pillar of the house. The roof was lined with individual rafters and covered with wide wood boards. Solid, light gray Spanish style roof tiles were secured into place. The building of the small house took no more than three weeks, but they had to wait for the well installers to dig and hook up the water pump system. The local electrician had to connect the main wires to the electrical box right outside of the kitchen.

I was impressed that, as a farmer, my

grandfather did most of the work with assistance from only a few individuals—he knew how to line all the in-house electric wires and plumbing pipes, lay the roof tiles, work with the cement, install doors and sliders, and place the Japanese tatami (floor matrices) in the dining rooms and bedrooms. Although he did not teach me anything about how to build or remodel a house, I was inspired by his knowledge and skills that he so easily incorporated into building the new house. However, I could not believe how basic the house was compared to our previous home, which was at least twice as big and had a wraparound porch/walkway.

I gather he must have noticed that I had a puzzled look as I gazed at the house. He called me over as he sat down on his old chair that he used when he needed a brief break during his work on the house. He held my hands and said, "Hide Chan, I know this house is small. But don't be deceived by the size of homes. There are lots of people in big houses that are unhappy and dissatisfied with their lives. Remember, you can squeeze all the happiness into any size house. We will remain a wonderful family—just wait and see." Such reassuring words with his confidence helped me to change my perspective on the house, small, but it was for all of us.

As the house was being completed, my grandfather sat me down again and told me that, "Before I forget to tell you, you should avoid committing your knowledge and skills to a single area. Just knowing all about farming work may be fine, but life calls for many other sets of knowledge and understanding how to apply them. In other words," he said, "you should be exposed to many different sets of things that you can do on your own, such as knowing how to work on plumbing, electrical wiring, installing windows, brick laying, cement work, repairing the leaking roof, landscaping, flower planting, and others. You should also be knowledgeable about music and art appreciation."

He also pointed out that knowledge could also be gained through reading books on geography, world culture, history, and the latest scientific discoveries. By the time I become a working professional, I should also know enough about economics and how it will affect my family's financial status.

After we moved into the new house, all of us went back to farming work. As I was helping him work on his peach plots, I noticed that he still practiced the tradition of individually wrapping peaches, which required such a huge amount of time. On average one tree produces four to six bushels of peaches annually. Imagine how much time was needed to fold small newspaper bags, cover all the peaches one-by-one before they start to mature, and take the bags off during harvest time. I asked him why it was worth it to wrap all those peaches. He lectured to me that this method had three advantages: (1) the peaches' skins remained soft at harvest time; (2) it prevented bugs from attacking and damaging them; and (3) the fruits did not need to be sprayed with chemicals. Grapes also were covered with somewhat larger bags to ward off insects, avoid the need for chemical sprays, and protect them from Japan's relentless rain. Exposure to moisture before harvest can cause mold and rot which make the grapes inedible and worthless.

Because Mas and I helped grandfather with his farm work, we learned how to grow rice, vegetables, and fruits. He also made us watch him work on his flower garden, located just outside of the house facing the living room that could be seen by opening the sliding doors. He planted annuals and perennials and beside them several shrubberies that produced bright yellow, red, and white flowers during the spring and summer seasons.

Just beyond the flower garden, we could see the Pacific Ocean about 20 miles down from the elevated lot on the hillside that our house stood on, facing east. My grandfather had specifically built the house to enjoy the view. The only liability was the typhoons that blew against our house directly from the ocean side during July and August. Fortunately, the house was never seriously damaged.

As I turned 13 years old

When I finally turned 13, my grandfather formally sat me down with him and started talking about life lessons, referring to his Words of Understanding that he kept in a notebook. This small book was about a half-inch thick with pages of notes like a reporter's handbook that's used for newspaper journalism. As he flipped through the notebook, I noticed that some of the words and sentences were crossed-out and rewritten. Even though at that time many of his instructions were not well understood by me, during later years I recalled the essence of his teachings. They awakened me with impressively useful perspectives. As presented in the following chapters, his invaluable messages became my guide as to how I should view my life and focus on the right missions during my formative and adult years in the US.

Chapter 5

SCHOOL AND CHURCH DAYS IN JAPAN

URING THE LATE 1950s in Japan most Catholic families' four-year-olds began Catholic preschools. Preschool teachers didn't teach numbers and letters because parents were expected to do that at home. Instead, the young students learned basic social skills like how to listen, pay attention, cooperate with others, and show respect to the school's teachers and administrators.

When I was 5 years old and my brother was 4, we attended a small kindergarten school run by the Catholic Church with about 10 children in our class. I didn't realize it at the time, but as an adult I realized that the teachers treated me with extra kindness and deference—I believe because my grandfather earned considerable respect as an esteemed member of the Catholic Church. I also think they knew we didn't have any parents and that may have led to "favorable" treatment as well. For instance, I had trouble falling asleep during our group naptime, so the teacher let me play by myself in a separate room until nap time was over.

Another time, during our daily break from classroom time, I was riding a bike by a cemetery near the school. Suddenly, my brother pushed my bike hard. I lost control and crashed into a tombstone, knocking my forehead into the stone. My brother told me later that I tumbled unconscious to the ground and bled profusely. In a panic, Mas ran to get the teacher—who also panicked because I remained unconscious and bleeding. She told my brother to get the French priest (who was head of the church and school). He instructed the teacher to clean the wound and cover the bleeding.

When I woke up I was in a hospital about 20 miles away from the church in the city of Ukuhashi with my grandfather, the priest, and head teacher peering at me. Again, due to my grandfather's stature at the Church, everyone must have dropped what he or she was doing and immediately rushed to get me medical treatment. This was unusual since the head priest would rarely accompany a kindergarten child to a hospital. That would be the head teacher's responsibility. In retrospect, serious injury to a kindergartener is bad news that the head priest likely did not want to be associated with for public image reasons. I still have the scar on my right upper forehead from the bicycle accident.

After kindergarten, my brother and I attended the local public elementary and junior high school. All of us attended school 6 days a week—and yes, we went to school on Saturdays, as well. School started at 8:30 AM and ended at 4:30 PM, but students would have to arrive about a half hour earlier. Before the first period, we had what they call "asanokai," or morning meetings, which focused on any issues or events of the day, plus any announcements from the homeroom teacher. But my brother and I were always there even earlier than required because my grandfather emphasized the importance of always being early.

He would always tell us, "If you arrive on time, you're late."

My grandfather had the 10-minute rule. He insisted that we should allow an additional 10 minutes before every task—going to bed, getting up, getting dressed, leaving for school—always arrive 10 minutes early to class, church, and other events. The way he explained it was that just 10 minutes made a huge difference in your demeanor. When you're late, you feel rushed and anxious; you lose your composure and can become impatient. When you have 10 minutes to spare, you're rewarded with self-confidence, grace, and dignity. The two worlds are very different.

Elementary school days

What I remember most about our elementary school days is how teachers continually emphasized the importance of learning about being good to others, and how bad behavior should be avoided and shamed by all of us. Japan is a small country with a huge population density—12 times more people per square mile than the US. If one-half of the US population were squeezed into the state of California, the population density would be about equal between the two countries. So Japanese kids aren't exposed to exams and tests until they're in 4th grade. Instead, early schooling prioritizes developing students' manners and character.

Young students are taught how to be generous, empathetic, respectful, and compassionate to others. They are also taught to develop a caring bond with nature and wildlife creatures and are informed about the importance of clean water and air for their healthy survival. Lessons on math, language, science, and other subjects remain as just basic reviews. We all wore uniforms throughout our schooling, which, according to my grandfather, was intended to remove barriers and help promote a sense of equity and togetherness among the students.

A field trip (I'm on far-right side touching my knees)

He also noted that the required school uniforms encouraged us to pursue self-expression through avenues other than our clothing. As he saw it, the uniforms ensured students' attention would be channeled toward learning and developing, not dressing up or superficial things such as the way we looked.

As a 5th grade student, one of my most memorable classes was Home Economics. All students (male and female) learned to mend clothing and sew patches and buttons. We also learned how to cook some fairly good dishes above and beyond the typical Japanese soup and salad options. Most boys enjoyed cooking sessions because we got to test and sample the dishes we all made.

One of the dishes I learned—a beef curry with vegetables and rice—became my specialty, and I still make it to this day. At the time, it became one of my family's favorite meals. They would often request that I cook it. I felt good and empowered about being entrusted as a young boy to cook and please my family.

Personal effort

Unlike Mas in junior high school, I did not make new friends. I simply came home from school uninterrupted and did my homework immediately to prepare for the next day.

I was feeling frustrated and angry at being left without parents. My life in those days was dull and unexciting. Only studying allowed me to escape to a separate island to recuperate from feeling deprived and unworthy, and I somewhat diffused the emotional suffering and pain I was feeling at that time. But the big benefit of my focus on studying was that I was prepared when it came time for exams.

I do not fondly remember any teachers enough to even recall their names. But I do recall the lessons our principal imparted. Our principal was a slightly overweight, short person. He was noticeable because of his large bald head and because most Japanese people (especially during those days) tended not to be overweight. Every Monday morning at the large front field of the school with all students neatly lined up, he would stand on a small platform with a microphone and would speak to the entire student body about the students' missions related to learning and studying (e.g., importance of engagement to learning, continual thinking about what the knowledge content means, generating questions to ask the teachers, etc.) and proceeded to introduce a concept of the week (typically a word reflective of a personal characteristic) for us to further analyze.

After his 30-minute speech, we went back to our homeroom and discussed that week's selected concept; how it related to our attitudes, how a person could show such a quality, or how we would know when we saw it in action. The lesson was supposed to help us practice humanistic qualities like compassion and avoid bad ones like greediness. The concept of the week remained written in large kanji—Japanese language symbols that represent ideas or meaning—on the blackboard for everyone to see for the entire week.

Even 60 years later, I still remember some of the humanistic concepts he instructed us to assess such as: *jiketsu* (自決) "self-determination," *nasake* (情け) "compassion," *kanzen-sei* (完全性) "integrity," *don yoku* (貪欲) "greediness," and *itsuwari* (欺瞞) "deceit."

The principal would also talk about highly successful alumni from our school or nationally adored or well-known individuals in Japan. For example, once he told us about a successful alumnus who became the CEO of a bank and how hard he studied math in school as a student. This dedicated, "warrior learner" showed up every day to school an hour earlier than others to review his math and other textbooks; the principal told us.

I only half-listened to these speeches, but they imparted a consistent message about the value of giving your best effort, one that aligned closely with one of my grandfather's biggest lessons. The effort you put into achieving a goal—not whether you've achieved it—is the most important thing in life. The importance of individual effort was emphasized above success, especially during my growing-up years within Japanese culture.

As my grandfather explained it, achieving something great is wonderful, but not as noteworthy as the intensity of your determination and focused willpower to give your best to reach the goal.

> He firmly believed that "the scale of personal effort is an index of one's greatness."

Often in our conversations he would say, "Do your best!" (Ganbate!). And instead of saying goodbye as I departed to my school, he would always say to me, "Ganbate!'

Learning about respect

Unlike in some other countries, teachers in Japan are highly respected by society and their students and viewed as a nationwide paragon. Teachers are required by law to be highly paid compared to other civil servants. Because of the respect they're afforded, most Japanese teachers remain in the profession until their retirement.

We were taught from an early age to show respect whenever we interacted with our teachers. Whenever a teacher entered the room, the students would stand and bow in unison. All teachers' assessments and opinions of us as a student (our academic strengths and weaknesses) were taken seriously with no disrespect. Teachers emphasized the importance of personal effort (e.g., the importance of engaged focus, continual practice or reviews, and knowledge of the content). Our top-performing students were always pushed to do more. Being a straight A student was simply not good enough—there was more room for further improvements. If one was blessed with high IQ, you had to work even harder than others to capitalize on your blessing. So being a top student was meaningless unless you continually committed yourself to dedicated and targeted personal effort. But the rigid school culture came with liabilities, too.

Once, I got in trouble simply for walking past a teacher I thought was taking too long to leave the doorway. As soon as I stepped in front of him, he immediately yelled, "Just a second, young man!" and told me how disrespectful it was for me to walk in front of him. He punished me by taking me out to the hallway and smacking me across the face. My nose started to bleed. As if that wasn't bad enough, he sent me home with a note to my grandfather, who punished me again. "Never forget," he told me, "Teachers are walking saints with profound knowledge." Maybe that's one of the reasons why my grandfather always wanted to be a teacher—besides the fact that they always came to school well dressed. Still, even some of the strictest and most frustrating teachers were able to impart important lessons.

One especially difficult teacher taught one of my math classes. When we completed his tests, he would check the answers in front of us and tell us how many we got wrong—

but he wouldn't tell us which ones. We would have to re-do all of the questions carefully to figure out and amend the incorrect answers. It was difficult, but the class taught me that exam completion speed was not nearly as important as its accuracy. And the teacher's tactic ultimately allowed us to earn a higher score in the end.

Classroom with teacher
https://mainichi.jp/english/articles/20181113/
p2a/00m/0na/005000c

Learning cleanliness

Japanese schools emphasize the importance of cleanliness. Consequently, visitors to Japan often declare how clean everything is, including our streets and highways, train stations, cabs, buses, subways, and public buildings. It's a cultural value that we learn from our youngest years.

Every student took their shoes off at arrival to the school and neatly put them in a huge shoe rack. Each box was printed with a unique number so students could remember which box held their shoes. It was a first-come-first-served arrangement so if you arrived early enough, you could choose your preferred box—usually at eye level, far right or left side. We also brought a second pair of lighter school shoes to wear in the classroom.

Every day after class all students were required to clean the classrooms, bathrooms, auditorium, and outside fields—a practice that continues in modern-day Japanese schools as well. Even homeroom teachers joined the school-wide cleaning ritual, and the practice helped us keep the school nearly spotless.

Cleaning by students (wearing the second pair of school shoes)

Thus, students didn't dare mess up the classrooms, bathrooms, or other school facilities because we knew we would be the ones cleaning them later. This practice taught us not only to value cleanliness, but also the power of collaborative comradery with a common mission, and the rewards that comes from teamwork. It also taught us to respect our milieu.

Although I understand that the publicly displayed student ranking is no longer practiced in Japan, the performance of the best students was aggregated and ranked for public viewing during my days. Out of about 300 classmates, a list of top 50 ranking individuals' names were listed on the hallway for everyone to view and revealed how hard good students were committed to learning. My academic performance was more than pleasing to my grandparents. I was often ranked in the top portion of the student body in 6th and 7th grade (I had the time to study). My favorite subjects during those days were Art, Science, and Geography, in that order, and I didn't really care about or enjoy math at the time.

In viewing the rankings of students by grades, I noticed that almost always more girls were among the top 50 ranking than boys even though the gender distribution was nearly equal. Thus, I learned to expect that girls would do better than boys in most of the hard subjects—math, science, geography, and biology, etc. Learning that girls were smart in school eventually led to my understanding of their significant strength and capabilities, an invaluable lesson about how everyone should see both gender groups as potentially invaluable assets and resources.

However, historically, Japan failed to capitalize on Japanese women's aptitudes until about years 1990 and later. The changes came about when American banks in Japan were hiring local women in various key positions, and who were significantly out-performing other banks that hired nearly all local male employees. Eventually, they started to realize that their gender related discrimination was costing their companies money. So, gender discrimination started to be addressed, and now companies are finally enticing far more Japanese women to stay employed and build-up their career. Fortunately, much earlier in my life I had gained awareness about gender equality, and I subsequently gained so much by working with super competent women in my later career.

Hard work even during summer vacation

Back in the 1950s, we went to school nearly year-round—with just one month of summer break in July and a few holidays from time to time. But even during our so-called summer break, we still had daily homework in every major subject, and students were given a thick self-study booklet to complete. On average during the summer, I spent a minimum of 2 hours each day reading and completing each study assignment. We had to turn in our answers on our first day back at school, so we would know where we needed to concentrate our academic efforts during the upcoming year. In recent years, Japan expanded student vacation periods off and on throughout the year, but they are still required to be in school 210 days compared to just 175 to 180 days in the US.

My grandfather was a board member of our grade school, so teachers again knew Mas and I didn't have parents at home. Unlike in Catholic kindergarten in grade school, I don't recall receiving special treatment from the teachers. This was a memorable difference for me. While my schoolmates were aware of our situation at home, to most of my class we were just normal kids being raised by our grandparents. The only thing that really made us unique was that we were Catholics. Only a few members of our community and their kids went to church every Sunday, all the Catholic holidays, and frequently on Saturday evenings as well.

Perhaps because most Japanese people are not immersed in the importance of religious practice, there was no bullying by the other kids because of our religious minority status. In contrast to its antagonism against Christians throughout history, Japan's post-WWII social and cultural interpretations of spirituality and dignified human behavior were taken more seriously by the people in general compared to the importance of strict mandates of religious worshiping practice. Japan became socially and culturally accepting of all religions and no longer mandated any specific religious practice. Thus, I personally seem to have learned naturally to emulate Japan's "modern" cultural perspective on religion.

This was a stark contrast to my family's history of dedicated Catholic practice, but I am convinced that a person can be as good as anyone by focusing on the humanistic philosophy, which was in part taught to me by my grandfather. Besides, for the way I treated my grandfather I gave up on the idea that I would qualify for admission to Heaven.

Fall sports festival

During the fall season, schools across the country held a school-wide sports festival called *undoukai* (運動会), where parents and relatives were invited to be spectators. Students were randomly divided into teams with colorful headbands and competed in sprint and relay races, as well as obstacle courses, tug-of-war, and other fun games. Local women's' dancing groups also performed traditional Japanese dances dressed in colorful kimonos with artistically decorated hand-fans, called *Uchiwa*. Their traditional dances were accompanied by loud festive Japanese music with huge drums.

Fall athletic festival
https://www.nippon.com/en/nipponblog/m00008/

My performance in the races was average at best. In contrast, Mas was in much better shape than me and often came in among the top three runners. But even though I wasn't the quickest, I always noticed how my grandfather was very focused on my effort—again, to him individual effort was the most important thing. And during those years in Japan, coming in first wasn't as big of a deal as it is in the US. The spectators would support the students coming in last, too, by giving standing ovations and clapping with screams of adoration.

During lunchtime, everyone sat on large blankets and ate special picnic food with their families, while some of the families, selected by the school administrators, sat at tables and chairs set up under huge tents by the school. Because my grandfather was a board member, we had a special table with a flower on top. An assortment of dishes was brought by families and presented for everyone (e.g., variety of vegetable sushi, beef-maki, which is vegetables wrapped with thin, cooked beef, or tempura vegetables, grilled teriyaki chicken, decorated hard boiled eggs, fruits, Japanese desserts, cookies, and several ramune and other cold drinks). After eating, we were allowed to visit other families to sample their leftover dishes and desserts. To me, that was the best thing about the fall athletic festival—a great lunchtime get-together with joyful families and friendly students.

Going to church

Our church, a structure with a gold Catholic cross at the top of its roof, stood by the foot of a mountain largely hidden from the main parts of the village. The church had about a 25 by 40-foot room in which congregants sat on the floor on their individual seating pillows. The priest's quarters were a separate small two-bedroom house with a bathroom and small classroom-size assembly room for holiday celebrations, the congregation's bible sessions, and other social events. To get to the small Catholic Church, it was a long walk—about 45 minutes each way, down narrow, rocky farm roads and hillsides—and when we got there, the sermons were mostly a bore.

The Catholic Church in Japan
https://japandeluxetours.com/destinations/nagasaki-oura-catholic-church

In those days, there were virtually no Japanese Catholic priests because of the small number of Catholics in Japan. Plus, there were no seminaries that existed nearby unless you lived in Nagasaki (about 140 miles away, which was a long distance in those days) where Christianity was first introduced. Thus, our church's head priest was a Frenchman who could hardly speak Japanese. He was perhaps 6 feet in height with a very white face and a short gray beard.

When he gave his sermons, virtually no one understood his heavily accented Japanese, and he often mispronounced words. To top it off, he gave the same sermon repeatedly, always mispronouncing the same words. The parishioners always looked bored and unengaged. However, Japanese nuns and the church's deacons held the bible sessions. Many devoted religious practitioners felt saved by these sessions and their after sermon informal discussions over hot green tea.

I was an altar boy, which was difficult with the French priest. Since I could never understand his prayer words, I often had to just keep looking at him for my service cue. Parishioners did the same to pray out loud, and very few sang along because virtually no one was familiar with the religious songs.

On one occasion, he forgot to cue me that I had to ring a small sanctuary bell, which was meant to symbolize the consecration signifying the holiest moment of the Mass, a symbol of reverent rejoicing. Right after the mass, as I was just about to meet my grandfather to head home, the head priest grabbed me and scolded "Aki reta yo! Nani o kangaete ita nodesu ka?" (Astonished! what were you thinking!). All I could think to say was "Sumimasen- Gomennasai" (I am very sorry, please forgive me). I felt as though I had just committed a serious crime that called for a severe reprimand and punishment. My grandfather already knew what had happened. He was also waiting for the bell to ring during the prayer. So he was also apologetic and assured the priest that I would never make the same mistake again.

In all honesty, I might've been daydreaming — which was easy to do during the boring mass. So I probably didn't notice his little signal to ring the bell. But I remained extra careful to ring the bell at precisely the right time.

Making a big mistake

Being parentless, I tended to be frustrated that my life was half-full. I wanted my mother and father at home, like other kids. I wanted to be able to hold their hands and hug them as I needed. In retrospect, perhaps because I was in such an emotional state, I might have been looking for a time to release my frustration.

One day as we were walking back from

the church with my neighbor's kids, the street split into higher and lower narrow pathways. From the top or bottom, you could not see where the others were, because of the thick and tall weeds and shrubberies covering both sides of the path.

Suddenly, I heard Takahashi Chan, my neighbors' son, shout "Bakatare, Hide Chan! (meaning, "you are stupid, Hide.)" In anger, my immediate reaction was to throw down a rock in the direction from where his voice came from - though I could not see where he was. Unfortunately, the rock hit his head and he started to scream. I got so scared; I ran home and acted as though nothing bad had happened. But that evening, Takahashi Chan's father came to our house and demanded an apology from me, not only directly to the injured boy but also to his entire family.

My grandfather was not only surprised and angry that I would do such a thing. He was sincerely apologetic to Takahashi Chan's father with remorse. After his departure, my grandfather looked at me with the eyes of fury and resentment. He immediately shouted "why?"

"He called me Bakatare," I told him. "I did not know that the rock would hit him."

In response, my grandfather taught me another valuable lesson.

"From now on, know this," he said, "if someone is nasty to you, only react at the same level of anger. If he is punching you, punch him back. If he is saying bad words, say bad words in return. But never go higher in your response."

My grandfather acknowledged that, if I was telling the truth, the boy did instigate the encounter.

"But your reaction should have never been to throw a stone — you should have just responded with your words," he added. "Promise me that you will follow this rule: Return fire only with the same level of ammunition thrown at you. That means if he had thrown a stone at you, you had every right to throw one back. But in this case, you had no right to throw the stone in reaction to his words.

Mas was nearby intensely listening and heard my grandfather's every word.

My aunt Seiko was also listening and her reaction was also a concern about my anger and behavior. She said, "I understand that your life is not as you wanted; especially when all others have what you feel is essential. But always remember that my adoration and your grandparents' love toward you two are unmatched by any of your friends' families."

She added: "You must focus on this ultimate truth: You are extremely lucky to be growing up with their genuine affection. And never forget the good side of your world and always appreciate the valuable gifts given to you."

Then Mas came and held my hand, showing me in silence that "we all love you." His gesture started to make me feel mended and revived.

That evening I walked over to the neighbor's house and apologized for my abhorrent behavior to everyone. Takahashi Chan did not look at me at all, but his father glared daggers at me. His mother, however, seemed to approve and accept my apology. "Please tell your grandfather that everything is OK," she said. "The injury was light and no hospitalization is needed." So I said again "Sumimasen- Gomennasai" (I am very sorry, please forgive me) and departed.

Takahashi Chan saw me days afterwards and apologized for calling me "Bakatare." He seemed sincere and wanted my forgiveness. That was an important exchange since there were only a few Catholic families in our town, so we needed each other's friendship more than other non-Catholic families.

Unforgettable slipup

One of the most unforgettable events that occurred to me during those years happened when I had just turned 12. In our community, most residents did not rely on the city's banks. They were located too far from the homes, typically in central parts of the city, so residents had to depend on buses to get there. Besides, official banks continually had high interest rates on loans and required significant amounts of paperwork to get loan approvals. So instead of joining a bank, my grandfather became a member of a community savings and loan group, which was entirely operated by local residents. This system was for members who were interested in being able to borrow or earn interest on their savings account.

Each month, all the members had to contribute a minimum amount of money as their savings investment. When a member needed a loan, they had to propose an interest rate that they were willing to pay for a loan. When two or more members wanted a loan, they had to bid their particular interest rate. The highest rate was used as the official rate. In all cases, however, members voted to approve or disapprove the proposed interest rate. Thus, if you seriously needed a loan you had to bid a high enough rate of interest to secure their approval.

One July day, my grandfather was tied up with some work on the house and wanted me to take the monthly loan payment to the community savings and loan meeting and tell them that he would attend the next month's meeting. He gave me an envelope with the payment enclosed (about the equivalent of $50 or so) to walk about 3 miles to hand it to the members in the meeting. When I arrived, the envelope was missing. It was not in any of my pockets. I started to cry as I told them that the money was missing.

I immediately noticed that some of the members' reactions (written on their faces) were disbelief, suspiciousness, and distrust. The chairman of the savings and loan association walked over to me and patted-down my pockets to make sure that the envelope was missing. Then, he reluctantly told me to tell my grandfather that the monthly payment was due by tomorrow, and if the payment was late, a penalty fee would be added.

I ran home crying. I told my grandfather that I had lost the payment envelope and explained that the chairman demanded payment by the next day. After checking my pockets, my grandfather warned me with fierce eyes and in a loud voice, "If you are telling a lie, you will be sent right to jail." I was obviously in shock and distraught that no one seemed to believe that I had lost the envelope. Everyone's first suspicion was that I must have been hiding the envelope.

Early in the morning the next day, the town's police chief came to see me. He directed me to follow him to the police station for questioning. I explained exactly what had happened; the envelope was lost when I got to the meeting. Then he repeated what my grandfather had already told me: "If you are lying, you will go to jail." He then told me to follow him to see the actual jail cell, which was being occupied by a scary looking man who must have been homeless. I noticed that he had wet himself. I was scared out of my wits looking at the man, who had a bloodstained face, perhaps due to his resistance to being arrested.

As I was being led back to the main office, I was surprised to see my grandfather waiting to meet with the police chief. He then proceeded to hug me and said, "Everything will be all right now. A lady found the envelope, and after hearing about the episode, she immediately came to our house to return the envelope with all the money still untouched." I was so relieved but couldn't stop shaking for some time. Then the police chief said, "I'm sorry you had to go through this. You will be OK; no need to worry."

My grandfather again hugged me and said, "I'm sorry that I did not believe you, even though I know that you are a good boy." I remember responding: "I'm sorry too, this would not have happened if I had been more careful with the envelope."

I further realize that this experience validated how much I was loved and accepted by my family even when I made serious mistakes. An invaluable exposure to how my family allowed for redemption— a distinct show of compassion that enhanced my heartfelt appreciation of their caring and loving actions. After I moved to the U.S. I came to an even greater appreciation of the love and acceptance I enjoyed from my family growing up in Japan. I faced some major challenges learning to fit into American schools and live with my new family.

Chapter 6

SURVIVING THE FIRST TWO YEARS IN THE USA

WHEN WE FINALLY arrived from San Francisco, I was pleasantly surprised by the size of my mother and stepfather's two-story brick house. It was much larger than typical houses in Japan. It had three bedrooms, a kitchen, living and dining room, and an open basement. As we entered, I was glad to see a TV, an upright piano, a large couch, and two soft chairs. I noticed that there were no pictures of my brother and me. In Japan, our house had several pictures of my mother in our bedroom and in the dining room.

My mother excitedly said in Japanese, "Follow me to your bedrooms!"

Our stepfather, yelling, immediately corrected her: "No Japanese in this house! Speak English!"

We followed her in silence. I was impressed that Mas and I had separate bedrooms and that we each had a small desk and closets. In Japan, my brother and I always shared one bedroom. In our new home, the bathroom was in the center of the house, while in Japan, our bathroom was in the corner of the house.

My mother whispered in Japanese, "I am so happy that finally we can live together. When Bill goes to work, we can speak Japanese (Nihon go) so I can answer any questions or concerns you may have."

At that moment, I could see on my brother's face a look of distress, fear, and helplessness. Later, he whispered to me how he was upset that we couldn't speak Japanese, even among ourselves, when we still didn't know English.

As I unpacked our suitcases, I began to cry when I realized that my father's record album (by Eugene Ormandy's Philadelphia Orchestra, which was recorded in the late 1930s) that Seiko had given to me was missing. I had buried it in the large suitcase and nothing else was missing, but it was gone. It could have been stolen on the ship, but I believe that Uncle Mituki took it when he checked the suitcases just before our departure. The album was the only thing I had that was my father's. I realized that now I had nothing that symbolized my father's personal position. I envisioned Mituki simply removing the album with no regard for the connection it offered me to my father. I felt seriously violated, saddened, and angry — I was filled with an intense hate of Mituki and his disdainful, uncaring attitude and actions.

I quickly put away the rest of my clothing and went to check how Mas was doing. He was sitting on his bed crying. He muttered in Japanese, "I don't understand why I'm here. I was so happy with everything in Japan, my grandparents, friends, school, and Aunt Seiko." This is when I finally realized that I was only selfishly thinking of what I wanted all along while neglecting the magnitude of Mas's emotional distress and calls for help. My grandfather had emphasized that I was responsible for Mas's welfare and contentment, yet I was seeing him heartbroken and in turmoil. I couldn't think of a word to comfort him. I felt guilty and hopeless, sad, and uselessly trapped. All I could do was to sit beside him and cry with him.

A few minutes later, my mother called,

"Hide & Mas, Hide & Mas! " So, we went downstairs and noticed that the TV was on.

Bill wanted us to see the Pirates' baseball game. He kept repeating "The champion, Pittsburgh Pirates!" We didn't know this until later but during the previous year (1960) the Pittsburgh Pirates had won the World Series by beating the New York Yankees. Bill was a big Pirates fan and so he was excited about seeing the Pirates play. Watching the TV, I noticed how relatively quiet Pittsburgh fans were compared to the much noisier Japanese baseball fans. Japan's games typically included half-dozen or more drumbeats, chanting that grew continually louder, and everybody jumping up and screaming when a ball was hit. Before the end of the 7th inning, mother told Bill that she wanted to take a picture of us dressed-up to send to Japan. She had already bought two jackets, ties, and white shirts for us to wear, which were mainly for going to church and other formal events.

Photo at house here with Mother

Awful dinner

My mother cooked and prepared dinner as we continued to watch the game. Our first dinner was some chicken dish with potatoes, carrots, and some green vegetables. I remember this because we could not eat it beyond our initial bites. We realized soon that my mother was a horrible cook—essentially due to learning how to "cook" from Bill. All the dinners were strictly American – meat and potatoes with some limp vegetables. Even though she knew how to cook Japanese dishes well, Bill disliked Japanese dishes. To swallow my mother's dishes required using heavy doses of ketchup and large glasses of milk or lemonade. You can imagine how much we longed for Japanese dishes.

For some reason, Bill believed that Japanese food was inferior and bad for your health. Later, I realized that Bill wasn't willing to give Japanese cooking a try because of his disproportionate ethnocentrism. He firmly believed that American dishes and American ways were the best by far in the world-especially compared to Japan.

To add to the tension and unpleasantness, we had to listen to Bill yell as we were struggling to eat our food: "Right now, people in India are starving; finish your dinner!" This was the opposite of what I had learned about dining etiquette. In Japan, the belief is that when your stomach is full, you should simply stop eating. In fact, eating less is better than eating too much. Forcing children to eat everything on their plates was another of his American norms.

Our neighborhood in Eastwood

Our home in Eastwood was located about fifteen miles from downtown Pittsburgh with no minority residents residing in the community until we arrived. Eastwood was an orderly town of about 5,000, which included a public library, an exclusive country club, several restaurants and drug stores, and Catholic and Presbyterian Churches. It was also home to the Community Symphony Orchestra, a small but highly active unit composed of young amateur musicians. The school system was ranked second best (among over 40 school districts) in the greater Pittsburgh region. The strict police department kept the community safer than others with their intense community patrol and monitoring. Streets were clean and in good shape, no potholes. The property values were higher than all other surrounding communities. Area realtors actively worked to keep the values at ascending levels by controlling and managing sales.

Eastwood had evenly divided numbers of upper middle-class and blue-collar families residing north and south of a railroad track, respectively. On the north side, upper middle-class residents primarily consisted of families with highly educated male heads of households (e.g., lawyers, engineers, accountants, and business administrators).

Two of the families owned companies that supplied rocket engine parts to NASA, and others had consulting companies for designing and building manufacturing plants. They were outlier families with huge mansions staffed with butlers, in-house workers, landscapers, and limo drivers. In contrast, families that resided on the lower south side of the tracks were mostly employed by the steel mills, the retail industry, or in support services for nearby manufacturers and business offices in the Greater Pittsburgh area.

Looking at the cars in the driveway, it was clear who lived on which side of the tracks. Upper middle-class families drove Cadillacs, Lincolns, Buicks and foreign sedans or sport cars compared to four-door Chevys, Fords, Dodges, and a bunch of older cars of the blue-collar families. Our stepfather owned an old subcompact Ford Falcon, silver with a 4-cylinder engine, which was not at all fancy looking. That's the typical kind of car a man could afford when he worked for the Steel Mill in the Hot Mill Section, where melted steel was converted into large steel coils or sheet plates.

We had a public park only two blocks from our house with a playground designed for young children, a baseball field and basketball court. The park provided play areas for organized T-ball, softball, and junior league baseball and basketball games. During warm summer evenings, this field was also used for showing family movies.

Meeting new friends

Soon after our arrival, our mother encouraged Mas and I to walk to the nearby park and try to make some new American friends. We were very reluctant because we did not speak English well enough to have a conversation. We only knew a few basic words. But after several weeks we finally decided to walk over to the field when I noticed that our stepfather was annoyed that we just sat around at home day after day.

So, with our mother's help, Mas and I prepared a small card to carry with us. We hand wrote our names, address, telephone number, and a note that said, "Please help us get home, thank you." The cards were for if we were to get lost in places other than at the playground or close to our house. With Japanese-English dictionaries in our pockets, we walked over to the field.

Immediately, several boys surrounded us. Some of them already knew that we had just arrived from Japan. I said, "Hi, my name is Hide (pronounced Hee Dee) and this is Mas." They introduced themselves and one boy asked if we played basketball. I told them no, since our school in Japan did not teach us basketball.

"How about baseball?"

I said, "Yes, Mas can play good."

"Ok, you want to play baseball?"

Mas said "OK."

As I had expected, on the first pitch Mas hit the ball into left field for a double. His physical fitness and speed paid off. I didn't do so well. I batted the ball near the pitcher who threw me out at first base. We played all afternoon. When the large clock hanging on the park's bathroom building struck 5:00 p.m., we all said goodbye and started walking home.

One kid shouted, "Good game. Play here tomorrow?" We nodded, even though we didn't know exactly what he was saying. But looking at his facial expression, I surmised that he wanted to meet and play again.

As Mas and I walked home, he was smiling and said to me that meeting the neighborhood kids and being able to show his baseball skills made him feel good. The kids made him feel worthy and not so different from them—a Japanese kid but athletically talented and skilled. He sensed that his good feeling was especially confirmed, as it was the best player who shouted, "Good game, play here tomorrow?"

I did not know anything about basketball, but I wanted to learn to play the game. The next day several kids were already playing and so I went by the cement court to watch. It was quite clear that tall players had a definite advantage. However, I noticed that if you can fake well, anyone could score against even far taller players. After watching them play for 30 minutes or so, one of the players asked me, "Do you want to play?"

I said, "No, I don't know how. I watch."

His response was, "OK, but here is another basketball, try dribbling the ball."

I did but it was quite difficult at first. I still liked watching the guys play and tried to memorize all the moves. At the end of the game, a guy came over to me and said, "Hi, my name is Jeff Bailey, what's your name?"

I said, "Hide, pronounced Hee Dee."

He said, "How do you spell that?" I told

him and his response was a simple "OK." He could tell that I was interested in basketball and said, "Here take this basketball and practice your dribbling at home. You can bring it back to me tomorrow." So, he handed the ball to me. By showing me how to dribble, I understood that he wanted me to practice dribbling so I could play with the guys. I did not understand that he was offering me his ball until he handed it back to me twice as he and the others were walking away from the court to go home. He repeatedly said, "See you tomorrow. Take the ball and practice dribbling."

I practiced dribbling and liked it very much. Using my broken English but aided by my dictionary, I asked my mother to ask our stepfather for several things, "Baseball, bat and gloves for Mas, and basketball for me." We already had our white sneakers. Bill said OK, but he wanted us to do the following chores: (1) cut the front and back lawn once a week all year except during the winter season; (2) every Friday, wash the car and wipe-dry it; and (3) after dinner wash all the dishes and put them away. You can take turns cutting the grass and washing the dishes. We were happy to do those chores. In fact, we did even more chores for our grandparents in Japan without earning spending money, like weeding the rice field all day, cleaning around the house, and bringing firewood back from the mountain about 3 miles from the house, and helping him fix the house (e.g., doors, sidings, and even changing the roof tiles). Working hard was not unfamiliar to us at all.

Jeff Bailey seemed interested in helping me learn how to play basketball. He asked me to meet him after dinner so he could teach me how to do lay-ups (right and left sides), shoot foul and jump shots, and how to steal the ball from an opponent. He also showed me how to pass the ball, direct and straight pass or bounce the ball close to a teammate. He said: "Practice, practice, and practice your shot!" So, I did. After dinner, I practiced intensely for several weeks until kids started to notice my ability to dribble.

With Jeff's assistance, I was eventually included in games with the other kids. Even though I was still learning the game, I felt that I really liked basketball. I noticed how it requires teamwork to get the ball to your teammates for open shots. Also, I liked faking out other players to get an open shot. But more than anything, I appreciated having a friend who took an interest in helping me to fit in. It was then that I finally started to feel like Mas and I might have a chance to be alright.

As I got to know several neighborhood kids, I also began to understand my grandfather's advice on aligning companionship with good friends who will magnify your joy and help defuse your sadness. It is not the number of friends that is important but the quality of these friendships. Thus, I felt good about Jeff's kind gesture to teach me to play basketball. Even though I was not a good player yet, playing with him made the game even more enjoyable and gratifying. I kept practicing basketball all summer and ended up wearing out the ball. Seeing my basketball with visible internal cords, Jeff pointed out the ball was for indoor use, not outside use. My stepfather was glad to buy me another ball (this time an outdoor basketball) because I think he wanted us out of the house and meeting as many neighborhood kids as possible.

Initial school experience

Forty-three days after our arrival from Japan to the USA, Eastwood School opened for the fall term. Mas and I were enrolled in 7th and 8th grades, respectively. We were very scared that we now had to somehow survive in an all-English-speaking school and take subjects like reading and writing, history, science, and math.

A week before the opening day, our stepfather took us to school to meet the principal and homeroom teachers. I understood very little during the meeting other than that they seemed to be welcoming our arrival. Bill also wanted us to know the directions to the school since we had to walk there and back every day. It was about a 10 minute walk so the school was not far at all compared to our school in Japan, which was about a 45-minute walking commute.

The first day of school was a disaster. I did not know that after meeting in my homeroom we had to go to another classroom after each period — this was different from Japan, where teachers walked to classrooms. I followed my classmates, but some split to another classroom so I had no idea where I should go. I just stood in the hallway until a teacher came by. There was a moment of embarrassment when I arrived late and just about everyone (all white students) looked at me. I sat at the closest open chair with a desk and the teacher introduced me as a new student from Japan. I understood this because she included the words "welcome" and "Japan." She then said, "Do you want to say something to the class?" Looking intently at her face, I could tell she was asking something. I said, "I cannot speak English, learning." The class was totally useless; I had no idea what the teacher was saying. I could only follow along in the textbook by looking at my classmate's book and trying to figure out the right page by matching mine to his textbooks' page number.

Welcome to second grade!

I was assigned to a second-grade English class by the principal who apparently thought that my learning English could begin at this level. I was able to decipher where the classroom was, but as I entered the room, I immediately noticed the second graders' facial expressions. They looked surprised and giggled. I gathered that most of them had never met someone from Japan. The teacher pointed towards the empty desk at the back of the classroom. I tried to sit in the chair, but it was much too small. More giggles followed. Their desks were built for 50-pound 2nd graders, not for 90-pound 8th graders. I had to remain standing in the back of the classroom and take notes.

Eventually, I was given a chair to sit, but no desk was ever brought. Second grade English was still very difficult for me after only 50 days in the U.S. According to the teacher's note to my parents, I was reading about 20 words per minute with often-wrong pronunciations. In comparison, typical second graders were reading 60 to 80 words per minute. The note indicated that unless I improved by the end of semester to at least 60 words per minute, I would flunk the English class.

At 11:45 a.m., Mas and I were finally able to meet to go home together for lunch. I asked him how it went, and he said, "We will never make it in this country. I have no idea what the teacher is saying, I could not read the textbooks, and I don't think we will be able to do the homework correctly. We are doomed!" I felt the same way and felt like I was having a panic attack — my chest felt heavy with feelings of disarray and horror.

My mother had prepared a Japanese lunch for us and wanted to know how school went.

I responded, "I have never flunked a course in Japan, but I will here, maybe all of them."

Mas started to whimper "Why are we here?"

Then for the first time I saw my mother raise her voice in anger and shout, "Because you two are my sons!"

Mas looked at me in silence, as if to say, "Please help me."

My one-o'clock class was mathematics. I immediately noticed by looking at the textbook that I had learned similar content two years ago in Japan. So, even though Eastwood School was highly ranked in the Greater Pittsburgh region, my math knowledge was two years ahead of the class. I felt so relieved that math would be a manageable subject. Right after school, I checked with Mas about the math content and he agreed we were way ahead of our class's mathematics course.

Both of us were glad that we would no longer look stupid in school. When one cannot speak the language, kids can treat you like a slow and backward person. You sense this because they speak to you very slowly and loudly as if somehow that would help. But as soon as kids realized that our math abilities were far more advanced than theirs, we hoped that we would even be viewed as smart kids.

My next class was art. The art teacher, Mr. Miller told me he already knew about my arrival from Japan and my limited knowledge of the English language. I understood much later that he was explaining that any artwork I wanted to complete as the term project would be acceptable. If selected, it would be shown on our school wide exhibit to be presented to the school board, teachers, students, and their parents. The top three pieces would win an award. However, I understood that his course was focused only on watercolor, oil painting, and ceramics. He made it clear by pointing to samples of artwork as he spoke. I could tell from his demeanor and facial expressions that he was a kind and considerate person.

This class was encouraging; I liked art, especially my art classes in Japan. I had won third place among several hundred contestants in my school's watercolor painting contest in 6th grade, so I already knew some basic techniques (e.g., watercolor wash, wet-In-wet watercolor painting, under-painting, etc.). In contrast, I had no courses or experience learning oil painting or ceramics.

Manipulated by a bully

I felt very bad during the first week when one of my fellow students took advantage of my inability to understand English. One of the big bullies in the class (big Frank) approached me with a smile and asked me if I knew what the word "fxxx" means? How about "sxxx" or "Mother fxxxxxx"? I said no.

"Well then," he told me, "as a brand new student, you must say to our homeroom teacher 'Get Bent.'

"She will like it," he insisted.

"What?" I asked.

"He repeated, "Say get bent, Mrs. Shorewood."

So, as Mrs. Shorewood walked into the room, I stood up, bowed, and said, "Get bent Mrs. Shorewood, thank you." The entire class bellowed, laughed out loud, and some seemed to be in tears. Mrs. Shorewood was not amused. Her anger was clearly written on her face.

"Who taught you to say that?" she asked.

I immediately noticed Frank's hostile, intimidating eyes glaring at me. Obviously, by then I understood that I had said something bad.

"I'm sorry, speak no English," I replied. I refused to identify who taught me to say those words.

She escorted me outside the classroom and discreetly said, "No bad words in this school, you understand?" I said OK and nodded because I could tell that she was dictating something serious to me.

This was an ironic event because it is rare that we used bad swear words against each other in Japan. And if one says to a Japanese individual: "You mother XXXXXX!" in Japanese words virtually no one would understand that you are swearing at him. One of the most outrageously worst things one can say in Japan to someone is: "Baka-tare," which means, "You are stupid." So, after this experience, I realized it's best to stay away from Frank as much as possible.

Meeting Stella

Finally, the first Friday of the week came and I noticed that the kids were in a better mood because they were looking forward to the weekend. As I was departing to meet my brother to walk home together, a classmate from my homeroom came to me and introduced herself as Stella. I immediately noticed her beautiful blue eyes, porcelain-white face and blond hair- I thought, wow, she is so beautiful.

She said, "You live on the same street as me, Greenwood Avenue, right?"

I understood "Greenwood Avenue," so I said, "Yes."

She then responded, "I can help you with your homework. Do you have time this Saturday at say, 10 o'clock?" I gave my Japanese-English dictionary to her so we could better communicate. She pointed out key words, including help, homework, Saturday, 10 o'clock, and repeated "Your home."

After arriving home, I blurted out, "A girl named Stella, Saturday, 10 o'clock, do my homework!"

"What is her last name," mother asked.

"I don't know but she lives here, this street." I was so excited; I had a hard time falling asleep that night. Like my grandfather had advised, I kept telling myself to think about some simple things to fall asleep, but my mind kept switching back to her and her words spoken in such a kind manner. The next day, I woke up much earlier than usual and immediately checked my closet to decide what to wear. I wanted to look like an American teenager. I managed to find a sharp shirt. I waited until 9:50 a.m. to put the shirt on and new gray pants that were bought for school.

She came right at 10 a.m. and knocked on our front door. I opened the door, greeted her, but my mother interrupted and said, "Thank you so much for your willingness to help Hide."

Bill also pitched in and said, "I have seen you; you live several doors down, right?"

She said, "Yes, and my name is Stella Mead."

"Yes, your dad also works at Steel Mill, right?" Bill continued.

She nodded yes. As I watched her in conversation, again, I remember thinking how pretty she was in her white blouse and yellow shorts. Her long hair was perfectly shaped. We started with the history homework. She had completed the homework, so she simply explained the questions and her answers and kept asking "OK? OK?" She did the same with the reading assignment. I cannot recall the title of the short story, but she was so organized that she listed the theme of the content she derived and proceeded to connect questions with her answers. We spent about 45 minutes on the homework. Then, she started to ask me about Japan and what kids there enjoyed doing on weekends. She took my English-Japanese dictionary and pointed to the key words. I responded using the same method. She was surprised to learn that we had school sessions on Saturdays. Using my dictionary and broken English, I explained how much homework we had in Japan, much more than was given at Eastwood School. She looked at her watch and said, "I have to go, but we can meet as you need during the week."

These wonderful homework sessions continued the entire academic year. I still remember how helpful and patient she was with me. I felt so at ease with her. She often smiled and repeated, "You are doing well, Hide!" She was a "walking angel," as my grandfather would say, and I couldn't help but adore her and appreciate her kindness. I desperately wanted to hug her, but I did not want to take a chance that she may not appreciate it. She was too precious to lose.

Just as the school year was ending, Stella came to our house looking depressed and sad.

I walked out of the house with her and asked, "What's wrong?" She took my dictionary and guided me to understand that her family was moving to Kentucky. Her dad got a good job offer in Ashland as a foreman with higher pay. Her uncle and cousins also lived there. Her family planned to move by the end of summer or as soon as their house was sold.

Unfortunately, the house was sold within two weeks; as noted, Eastwood was a highly appraised community due in part to its great school system, safe neighborhoods, and well-maintained homes with clean streets. Less than a week later, Stella came over and told me that her mother was already in Ashland, staying with her uncle and looking at neighborhoods in which to reside. I was crushed that I may never see her again. My energy level plunged, I lost my appetite, and I had hard time breathing normally as I lay trying to fall asleep. I kept waking up feeling sad and disoriented.

Stella never came back to Eastwood. Bill wouldn't allow me to use our telephone for long distance calls. He said it was too expensive. Besides, it would have been too difficult for me to carry on a conversation without the use of my dictionary with her.

That year our only communication was a Christmas card. No communication followed. I realized later that this is another instance where I wished I could have heeded my grandfather's advice. He always encouraged me to maintain and nurture good friendships. See and talk with your friends often, he would say, and keep them aware of your life events and developments. I wish I could locate Stella to tell her how much her assistance meant to me and sincerely thank her—I regret never getting that chance, and even today (after 60 years) I still recall her compassionate voice and engaging smiles.

Flunking 8th grade

At the end of the academic year, even with the great scores I received on my homework assignments, and the A's I received in art and math, I was informed that I flunked the 8th grade and must repeat the grade next year. I was not surprised since my exam performances other than math were pitiful. Most of the time, I could not understand the questions. Teachers allowed me to use my English-Japanese dictionary during the exams, but it didn't help enough. Frequently looking up

English words delayed my ability to generate correct answers on time. Oftentimes, I could only finish just over one-half of the exam questions. When essay questions required my response, it was hopeless. I received an F in most of my classes, even in my second-grade English course.

I was surprised, however, that Mas passed 7th grade, even though his English was slightly worse than mine. My stepfather met with the principal about me flunking the 8th grade and was told that 9th grade was much more important and difficult than the 8th grade. Thus, they felt I needed more time to learn English before I entered the 9th grade. In retrospect, I believe that was the right decision. Especially when I found out that a foreign language course was required starting in 9th grade. Imagine if I was enrolled in a German class; I would not have known if the teacher was speaking in English or German.

In the following academic year, I ended up in my brother's 8th grade class. It was embarrassing for me, but it seemed to be no big deal to my new classmates. Perhaps, it was understandable to them that with limited English, it would be difficult to pass exams in required courses. They knew, however, that we were ahead of them in math, and so to them we were simply being challenged with limited ability to understand the English language.

Devastating letters from Japan

In August, about a month after Stella moved away, we received a letter from Japan informing us of our grandfather's passing. He had refused to take his blood pressure medicine or be admitted to a nearby hospital. I gathered that he felt it was too late for recovery and hospitalization was a waste of money. Our Aunt Seiko's letter indicated that she and my grandmother were at his bedside moments before he died. He, without words, stared into my grandmother's eyes.

> She said to him "I know you will be in heaven waiting for me. I will see you there. Thank you so much for our wonderful, happy, and good life. I will make sure that Hide and Mas will know that you passed with dignity, that you loved them and were very proud of them."

My mother, Mas, and I, sat together, crying, trying to comfort each other. His passing was immensely difficult for me as I lacked closure with him. I felt awful that we missed seeing him and sharing our feelings of love, respect, and gratitude. His passing overwhelmed Mas—he simply wanted to be left alone in his room and weep. Later that evening, he came to my bedroom and pleaded with me to arrange for our return to Japan. He wanted to visit our grandfather's burial site and tell him about our admiration and sorrow, and how much he meant to both of us.

I went to Bill with a promise to pay him back for our travel costs to Japan. However, he flatly denied this request. Bill felt that it was too late anyway and would cost much more than we could save and eventually pay him back.

About nine months later, we received another letter from Aunt Seiko. Our grandmother had died in an auto accident. A car had hit her, as she was crossing the street. Several months later Bill approved of our mother going back to Japan to visit the burial sites of our grandparents. We were again denied the visit for cost reasons. After our mother's return from Japan, I found out that Bill only approved of our mother's return to Japan to find out if any of us had received an inheritance from our grandparents (mainly their house and some farming plots, which were left unmanaged). However, our mother was informed that our grandparents' will of inheritance was being contested by Mituki in court claiming that we had no interest in returning to Japan.

Right after my grandmother's passing, Mituki had sent a special delivery letter to my mother asking if my brother and I plan to be returning to live in Japan, without explaining why he needed her response ASAP. Obviously, my mother had responded that we would all remain living in the US. Apparently, my mother's response was included in the Mituki's filing to a court with a request to the judges to transfer the inheritance to Seiko (his wife) who had lived with my grandparents longest until her marriage in 1960- last child of the grandparents to leave home. Thus, the court eventually approved the transfer of the inheritances as legally permissible because Mas and I had no plans to come back to Japan.

Therefore,my first two years in the US

were filled with unexpected sadness (i.e., my grandparents' passing), blessings (i.e., meeting new friends, Stella's assistance, and easy math courses) and challenges (i.e., English language and coping with limited ability to speak or write in English.) The academic year of our eighth grade ended with no flunking final grade (mostly D's and some As.) Thus, we were allowed to proceed to the 9th grade.

Chapter 7

SURVIVING HIGH SCHOOL YEARS

A T THE BEGINNING of 9th grade, we were informed by the principal we had to take required IQ tests. He summoned us to a conference room next to the principal's office. We nervously walked into the office with a huge desk and a man instructed us to sit on opposite sides so he could individually test our IQ. The principal apparently ordered this test since they were uncertain as to whether we may be suffering from learning disability or mental retardation. I noticed that no other students were summoned to take the IQ tests. As may be expected, our language limitation contributed to our IQ scores being less than 100 – both of our IQs were estimated to be around 85.

This event was memorable because an

IQ test was never issued to us in Japan. It was also worrisome too because I did not want to be told that we were mentally deficient. Among Japanese kids, being categorized as mentally deficient is the worst curse and every parent's nightmare. Thus, my official transcript indicating my IQ as 85 was painfully distressing, troublesome, and demeaning since I knew better—I was a good academic student in Japan. The last thing I wanted was to be called "baka-tare"-stupid.

That year, I enrolled in French class because some of my classmates told me that the teacher, Miss Davis, was the easiest teacher. But I hadn't yet mastered English, so I still had significant difficulties distinguishing between English and French words. Basic French words like Bonjour! (Good morning, hello), Pardon, excusez-moi (Pardon, excuse me), Je ne parle pas français (I do not speak French) were relatively easy. But when challenged to write sentences and paragraphs, I painfully struggled.

I prayed that I wouldn't end up with another F by the end of the term, but I also remembered my grandfather's teaching — that God is not there to give you things, only to help you work harder to reach your goals and to help you focus your efforts.

So with that in mind, I decided to double my effort in French class and practice with a portable tape recorder that I had purchased, along with a tape called "Introduction to French for Travelers." This paid off — I ended up with C- as my final grade. This grade felt like winning a huge contest. Other than my art and math grades, C- was the highest grade I earned in the previous years.

During the same academic year, I was encouraged by my gym teacher to work to get into far better physical shape. He was trying to organize a wrestling team and wanted me to join. Not only did he need more students to join the team, but also apparently he found out from other students that I was familiar with judo, karate, and kendo. Such knowledge and skill could put my opponent at a disadvantage in wrestling. However, I wasn't interested in joining because I was not fond of my potential teammates, who were big and arrogant and seemed like bullies. But while I was watching TV at night, I did push ups during commercial breaks — and it wasn't unusual for me to do as many as 160 push-ups every evening. The gym teacher's encouragement during his recruitment effort energized me to focus on getting stronger and in better shape.

Those informal exercises, combined with avidly playing basketball games, strengthened my physique. As a result, I won the school's annual 9th grade competition for the most pushups (67 in 60 seconds) and most one-handed pushups (30 in 60 seconds). I also took first place in rope climbing. I was able to climb up and come down on an exercise rope hung from the gym's ceiling about 30 feet high or so in 6 seconds. I believe such physical improvement contributed also toward building my figure as well. I noticed how some of my female classmates' eyes focused on my body as I entered class.

To my surprise, towards the end of the academic year, I won a top art award for my colorful ceramic vase. Some of the teachers said they had never seen such art — actually, that's because they were not familiar with art that had a Japanese flare. My art teacher, Mr. Miller was especially impressed with my color combinations — I used black, copper, and gray, instead of the light pink and dark green that my classmates were drawn to — and the curb-liner shaped geometric design that was somewhat common for Japanese art. Unfortunately, my ceramic vase was missing (stolen) just before the last day of showing. Believe it or not, I wasn't upset or angry much about the unanticipated occurrence. I thought I could create another one anytime. Besides, real joy was during the creation of the base- when it was completed, not as much.

Coincidentally, Mas, too, won his woodshop class's top award for building a night lamp that resembled a watermill with big wheels that spun, to emulate spinning by falling water. It was impressively good work of not only scaling the watershed parts so perfectly but also artistically carving the water flow marks and chimney built with stones. A light with a tiny switch also worked flawlessly. I definitely thought his creation was far better than mine. Fortunately, his piece was for the workshop contest, not the art contest, or he probably would've beaten me! Even after 60 years, he still has his prized watermill lamp in his position.

Sophomore year

On the home front, while my mother

might've been a poor cook, she was an excellent seamstress. She could sew just about any style of shirt, pants, and even suits and heavy jackets. In fact, my mother made most of her own dresses and even several of Bill's suits. So, Bill decided that she could further reduce the household budget by having her sew all of our school clothes. I saw this as an opportunity to choose my favorite style and color options for my clothes, as well as the fabrics. Bill said OK as long as they were cheaper than buying the clothes from a department store.

When I started 10th grade, I decided to dress distinctively from the other students to be noticed more as a unique artistic teen-ager instead of just a Japanese boy. For example, I selected a purple slim-fit shirt with an all-yellow collar, front pocket, and cuffs, or a black shirt with a white front pocket and cuffs, or all dark red shirts with yellow stitching around the collar, front pocket, and cuffs. While most students wore drab khaki pants, my pants were all black, dark blue, pure white, or dark brown, and all slightly tight fit.

Because of my unique attire, the principal once asked me, "Where did you get your school clothes?" I told him that my mother made them. I think he was surprised. I got the impression that he thought my clothes were too wild or out of the norm for school attire. He was stunned that my mother — who was from a traditional country — would approve of such conspicuous color combinations. However, that was all my doing and maybe because I liked them so much, my mother also said she liked them. In Japan men can wear, for example, dark purple pants with pink shirts and it is perfectly OK. In the US, such a combination could invite unflattering comments and false branding. Thus, I made sure that my clothes were never extreme combinations- just artistically presented.

During 10th grade, I became more confident about socializing with friends, mostly because of my improving English and how my classmates treated me as their friend. I was frequently invited to their birthday parties and get-togethers at the park, and holiday events at their homes. Passing the drivers' test and getting my license helped as well, especially for getting to know Deli, a stunningly upper-class student (in 12th grade). She was my good friend Jeff Bailey's older sister. With my stepfather's silver Ford Falcon, I often picked up Jeff and Deli and drove them to open house parties, basketball games, or around the neighborhood.

Deli not only had beautiful eyes, but she also had a kind demeanor as well. She always had something nice to say, and her frequent smiles made me feel at ease and peaceful. She was my first real crush that commanded my willingness to please her in any way she desired. Eventually, both of us felt that we could openly share our thoughts with each other. Once, we were driving around and Deli asked if I could stop at the drugstore because she needed to buy tampons — an untypical request for a young woman in the 1960s. She also had no problem telling me about how she would like to be made love to by a lover and would gladly lose her virginity. However, I don't think she realized at all that I wanted to go beyond being friends with her.

Unfortunately, she already had a boyfriend, who wasn't a great guy, in my opinion. He frequently drank beer and wine, often got into fights, and was arrested several times for being drunk. So, to my elation, his parents sent him away to a private school located near Philadelphia, about 300 miles away from Eastwood.

Due to his absence, Deli and I were able

to spend more time together. I frequently visited her home and we often spent time on her porch sharing Pepsi and talking about anything from gossip about classmates to fascinating facts about the universe and reaching the moon. When she bought a new outfit, she wanted me to give her my genuine opinion on how she looked. Being so pretty, however, she looked good in just about anything she wore.

Consequently, I dreamed about Deli breaking up with her boyfriend, who wasn't always nice to her. Because he drank so heavily, he tended to be a lover boy to other girls. When Deli got upset, he would always belittle her as a "pain the a**-bitch", and accuse her of always whining about everything. Ironically, he was also an extremely jealous type who often falsely accused her of lying and cheating. They argued so frequently that I wondered why she liked him so much. I felt his good looking and daring personality, which was attractive to some girls, was unjustifiable for her offering of adulation. He didn't appreciate her. My grandfather would not have approved of how she was being treated- with no sense of dignity.

We were close friends, but I was still

surprised that Deli asked me to the annual Girls Ask Boys Dance that year. In the days after she asked me, I was so nervous and elated that I couldn't eat or sleep much. I couldn't think about much else than about her. I was excited to go to the dance, but anxious because I didn't know how to slow dance. So I had to tell Deli — and thankfully, she was kind enough to invite me over to teach me. We practiced for several days and evenings until I felt more confident about going with her to the dance. When the night came, I wore a white jacket with a black tie and pants. She was in a beautiful red dress with red high heel shoes and her hair tied up with a red bow.

My solo picture at Girl Ask Boy Dance

She looked like Miss America, only even more gorgeous. However, she didn't want anyone to take our pictures, because she was afraid that her boyfriend would be enraged if he learned that she went to a dance with another guy. So my photos at the dance remained solo pictures of me and myself. Still, as I had anticipated, we had a wonderful evening of dancing. When she held me for a slow dance, I could feel the pounding of my heart and I did not want the music to end.

Mas became a tough kid

During my sophomore year, Mas also became more outgoing. He became popular among several tough guys, some of whom were avid smokers. He was well-liked because of his candidness and openness to share his thoughts, like how he hated his stepfather, disliked school, and his displeasure with how kids were treated by local police. Because he readily spoke his mind, he sometimes triggered some of his friends into arguments, threats, and name-calling. When those tough guys challenged him, Mas proved his strength and took no mercy when defending himself. Mas became known as a "tough guy" who knew how to fight using karate, which he had learned in the training facility near our house in Japan. He often visited his friends to lift weights and to check out their parents' swords (from WWII and apparently some of them were from Japanese and German soldiers), hunting knives and guns.

But he also had a few good friends who never got into troubles and hassles. He also kept up frequent communication with his half-dozen friends in Japan, who informed him of all the interesting developments in our hometown and updates about kids he knew.

One of the liabilities of being known as a tough kid is that other tough kids in nearby communities wanted to challenge him to fight. I'll never forget the horror I felt when Mas came home holding blood-soaked t-shirts to his head because two hoodlums from an adjacent community had attacked him with a pipe when he was in the men's room at a gas station.

Mas spun around and used his karate skills to defend against the hoodlums. Surprised, the guys fled when they realized that Mas was tougher than they had expected. He ended up with 13 stitches in his head and some bruises, but otherwise he was fine. Later his attackers ended-up in the Pennsylvania state prison because of their drug and assault-related crimes. One of them died soon after his prison release from a high-speed getaway attempt in a stolen car after crashing into a brick wall.

Junior year

My junior year turned out much better than I had ever expected. One day, while hanging out with friends drinking Pepsi in the park, I had an idea for how I could win the class presidency. It was kind of a ridiculous thought. There had never been a minority student as junior class president and Mas and I were still the only minority students in the entire school.

But I figured out a strategy to potentially win. Because our community was divided almost 50-50 between white-collar and blue-collar residents, I figured that I could win the presidency if my friends nominated two popular students from the white-collar group, who would then split the vote. Then, I could accrue enough votes by getting most of the blue-collar votes.

I discussed this plan with several of my blue-collar friends, and they thought the idea was cool. As I expected, the two popular students split primarily white-collar vote 35% and 25%, and I received the other 40% and won the election. When the results were announced, the teachers seemed surprised and somewhat concerned. I saw how the teacher who announced the results looked stoic, and not at all congratulatory toward me for winning the election. I believe he was concerned that a minority student struggling to speak and write in English had to present himself as class-president at all of the main events of the high school before audiences filled with dignitaries, teachers, and parents.

His look immediately reminded me of when I had tried to have my family join a local country club with various facilities for swimming, playing tennis, basketball, and bowling. Many of our classmates met there on weekends and vacation months to play with each other. When I went to the Club to inquire about joining the club, the managers seemed impassive and uninterested.

"Right now, the membership is full," he told me, "and so we cannot take in any new members."

He had no other encouraging words like, "try again in 3 months," "I will let you know when an opening comes up" or "I'll put you on a waiting list."

When I mentioned this experience to some of my friends, they got irritated and said that they would take me to the club as their "guest," starting the next weekend. When the manager saw me at the club, he seemed surprised, and not at all welcoming. I gathered that such a reaction is simply an innate reaction towards someone who is different. After all, my brother and I were not just the only minority members in our school but also in our community (including my mother). I cannot recall who said this to me now, but I was asked once by an adult community member, "How did your family end up in Eastwood?" At that time I did not completely understand the question, but I remember simply replying, "I don't know."

But as class president during my junior year, I wasn't too worried about racial prejudice. I continually reminded myself about the lessons my grandfather had taught me about leadership in his Words of Understanding:

> What is the most important factor for maintaining leadership? Trust others. How do you earn trust? By

practicing honesty, respect and caring towards individual members, and by solving problems with fairness. Don't forget to show an earnest recognition of the contributions made by others. Furthermore, arrogance and feelings of superiority over other individuals are inferior human traits. Arrogant people are desperately trying to hide their inabilities and uselessness by attempting to deceive others and hide their fraudulent self. So, when you meet arrogant people, have sympathy for their weakness and shortsightedness. Always practice being dignified with your words and actions and remain humble and respectful of all others.

One of my main tasks as class president was to help plan the junior prom. I led a planning committee that included the vice president, three additional students and two teachers. We chose everything from the venue to the buffet menu. Following our homeroom teacher's advice, we encouraged our class to invite their classmates to the dance — we wanted as many juniors as possible to attend this important and memorable event.

Since I would introduce the prom committee members and give a brief thank you speech, I realized that I had to bring a date. But it was a challenge to pick one of my female classmates to invite. Out of 78 students just about half were girls, but nearly half of the girls already had a boyfriend or were interested in other guys in our class.

That meant I had to select from the remaining 19 girls, and someone else had probably already asked nearly half of them. So, I had to work with the remaining 10 or so girls, which included those (or possibly all of them) who might be uninterested in being asked by me to the prom. I hurried and asked Pearl Valentine, who was the prettiest girl in our class. She already had a college boyfriend at Stanford University in California, but I figured it would be unlikely for him to travel all that way home just for a weekend, so she would be without a date.

Pearl was not only kind — she always had nice words and a warm smile for others — but she was also beautiful. What made her so special included her spiritual integrity (e.g., showing sincere good-will, good thoughts and kindness to others), and her high interpersonal IQ (e.g., always had nice words for others with sincere smiles), which were enhanced by her beauty and loveliness. I often saw her volunteering for several services to the needy, including assisting mothers' collection for March of Dimes, organizing Christmas gifts programs for children served by local non-profits, and social events for kids in the local school for deaf individuals. She was the only person in our class to learn tactile fingerspelling to communicate with deaf students. Guys often fought to sit close to her in our classes, because she brought such joy and delight to people around her. She was a perfect 10.

When I asked her to the dance after class one day, she told me she'd have to ask her boyfriend first — but she came back the next day and told me that everything was okay.

Our Junior prom with Pearl

I was initially excited, but that evening I started to feel somewhat uncomfortable that I was taking the most beautiful person in my class, inside and out, to our junior prom. I was aware of my minority status, and I worried people would make a big deal out of us being a mixed-race couple, especially considering that Pearl was a Miss America-level beauty. I thought older adults would disapprove, like the teachers, parents, and staff members of the club where the prom was being held, and at dinner just before the prom. So it was a mixed blessing - all good and all bad at the same time.

The night of the prom didn't go exactly as planned. The country club was decorated beautifully to suit the "Beyond the Mountain" theme with help from some parents who were professional interior decorators, so the set was perfect. However, the prom band was supposed to arrive to set up around 7 PM, so they could start playing by 8 PM. But no one showed up. The music committee started panicking and pointing fingers at each other.

Fortunately, one of my best friends, Mike, had just recently organized his own band called "Our Gang." At my request, he rounded up the rest of his group and within the next hour, they had set up at the prom, ready to play.

With Mike as lead vocalist, the audience was thrilled with the sound of the band. Some of my classmates asked me, "How did you pull this together?" "The band is great!" This was a huge relief- I thanked Mike over and over and said, "I owe you a big one- you are a great savior!"

But as the evening progressed, I became sensitive to what I thought were the judgmental facial expressions made by some of the people — mainly parents, teachers and other adults — watching me slow dance with Pearl. It seemed that they were looking at Pearl more than observing me. So, while we danced I was in two worlds at the same time: One of joyfulness, enjoying my night with Pearl and one of uneasiness, feeling the glares from adults.

Pearl seemed totally unaware that she was being watched. She seemed to be having a great time and was a wonderfully graceful and beautiful prom date. So, in hindsight, I may have been wrong — perhaps people were observing her for her beauty, not seeing her as an improper young person, as I had worried.

That night was "Our Gang's" first major debut under Mike's leadership. Mike was the lead singer and great vocalist. He brought his musical soul and spirit right to the audience's ears, and directly to the hearts of people who loved soul music and the Motown sound. He emulated songs by top artists at the time, like James Brown, the Temptations and Smokey Robinson.

Our gang - Mike is beside the drum

Prom attendants adored Mike too because he was a humble and well-spoken person, and not at all arrogant regardless of being such a talented vocalist. These factors contributed to all of us having a great time at the prom. And, more importantly, his last-minute help averted what would have been disastrous memories for my classmates, teachers and the principal of Eastwood High School and parents of the Eastwood community.

After they had been playing for a while, Mike asked me to be the electrical technician of the band. My job was to hook up all the wires between the amplifiers, speakers, microphones, guitars, and lighting, and to test to make sure all were in good working order. During the weekends, I attended Our Gang's shows at young people's dance clubs, enjoying their music and watching artistic all-girls young dancers of that time, many of whom were studying and hoping to become professional dancers. They were known in Pittsburgh as the best future dancers that showed off not only their unique dances for rock and soul music, but they also exhibited integrated snapshot versions of entrancing moves like salsa, foxtrot, waltz, and rumba.

As I intensely watched their moves, they danced even more intently with their cool and graceful sways and turns of their sensual bodies. One of my grandfather's comments applied well even to the young dancers: The best-kept secret to a woman's beauty is her "gracefulness," which is relevant to alluring dancing as well.

By end of junior year

By my junior year, I was doing okay in school, but I still got crushed in English class. That year, our teacher, Miss Island, assigned a small book entitled Ivanhoe by Water Scott. Miss Island said that the book was a great read for anyone who enjoys historical novels or adventure fiction, but as a student who was still learning English, it was astonishingly difficult to read. In just one paragraph of about 200 words from the first chapter, I had to use my Japanese-English dictionary to look up over 40 of them. For me to read and understand this book of 680 pages, it would have taken an enormous amount of time.

With grave apprehension, I wrote to my best friend in Japan what Mas had said to me on our first day of school: "We are doomed," I told him, lamenting, "we will never make it here in the USA. The English language is much too difficult." I sent this letter in 1966 to my Japanese friend Nakamura San — and 40 years later, when we visited him in Japan, he brought this letter to me to see again. Then he asked how I overcame my challenges with English. My answer to him was that I never overcame my inadequacy- I am still learning to speak and write better.

Miss Island was a very tough teacher. Mas and I ended up with Ds as our final grades. But I was thankful that it was not an F since I could not afford the time to read the entire book. I just focused on the first sentence of each paragraph, and then got Pearl to help me with the descriptions of the main characters and to understand the theme of the book.

In contrast to English class, I was pretty good at math and my ability gave me the opportunity to earn and save some money. Andy, Our Gang's bass guitar player, was a much better musician than 10th grade math student. When his mother found out that I was good at the subject, she offered me $1.50 per hour to tutor him, plus bonuses if my help raised his grade from a D. She offered me a $20 bonus if Andy got a C, $50 if he got a B and $100 for an A. Unfortunately, I only earned the $20 bonus, but my savings from this job amounted to about $100 during the 4-month tutoring period, which was a substantial amount back then. I simply saved the money for future expenditure. It felt great to know that I had that much money at my disposal and helped me to keep the money instead of wasting it on ephemeral leisurely items.

SAT test

During the winter of our junior year, we were told about the upcoming SAT test, which we'd have to take in the spring for admission to college. Just before school dismissal time, our principal came into my homeroom and instructed me to come into his office for a brief meeting. As I sat across from him, he asked how my English was coming along and how I liked the school in general. Gradually, he got around to his main point. He wanted to discourage me from taking the SATs. He suggested that I might be far better off as a plumber, auto repairman or a construction or steel mill worker. Such jobs don't require taking the SAT exam.

I was disillusioned at his suggestion. His administrative advice sounded demeaning and judgmental. I wanted to further capitalize on my abilities in math or art.

When I told my mother what the principal suggested, she was livid. She wanted Mas and me to become successful professionals with a college degree. She pointed out that "your father was a college graduate!" She insisted that both Mas and I sign up to take the SATs.

I later wondered if the principal was less concerned about our future and more worried that our SAT scores would bring down the school-wide average, which was, in part, used to rank high schools in the Greater Pittsburgh region. Losing the number two ranking would be an embarrassment for his board members and for stakeholder parents. Realtors, eager to keep property values high, would also be upset and could cause a commotion.

I took the SATs, and the principal's worries about my low scores were partly confirmed — I scored 276 on English, but did much better, 649, in Math. My senior year, my scores increased somewhat, to 302 in English and 696 in Math. Despite my poor English score, the school's ranking didn't change. Thankfully, Eastwood High school still remained the second best in the Greater Pittsburgh region. As we demonstrated that we were strong math students, our senior class's math teacher suggested to us that we might want to consider the engineering field, which required lots of calculations based on math.

Designing and building a go-kart

One evening we saw a television program that included a go-kart race and Mas and I were impressed. When we inquired about the cost of buying the go-kart, it was too expensive- well over $300 depending on the size of the engine and other options. So we decided to explore building one from scratch. We drew the go-kart design and asked our stepfather if he could bring home angled iron plates from his steel mill. He said he would but only because the security guard knows him as their union representative.

We cut the angled iron with a hacksaw to build a frame for the kart. With the help of the guys from our local machine shop, all the mounts and frame connections were welded. Although we did not know the machine shop guys, when they saw our go-kart design on the paper, they were amused and became interested in helping us. They estimated that as long as everything was cut to the specifications and ready to be welded, it would cost us $20 each- we thought that was a reasonable price.

Mas located a used 7-horsepower engine that he used in his go-cart, and I bought a used 10-horsepower aluminum engine that was originally mounted to a racing go-kart for mine. Both engines had their own gas tanks, as well as a centripetal clutch that engaged automatically to the sprocket that we designed to turn the rear tires. Altogether, building the go-karts required slightly less than $100 each for everything.

Our go-cart

This project reminded me of my grandfather's statement about the difference between knowledge and understanding. He felt that knowledge itself tends to be useless unless you can apply it for a useful purpose. He also had noted that lots of arrogant people may be knowledgeable, but they lacked understanding. We had enough basic knowledge of math but that did not guarantee that we could apply it to build a go-kart.

Figuring out the steering mechanism, determining the ideal location of the engine bay for connecting the chain links to the back wheels, how to mount front and rear brakes (at what angle and distance from the wheels) and what was the ideal length and width of the go-kart all required math and mathematical vision. In other words, by building the go-cart, we were challenged to demonstrate that we understood how to use our math. Thus, building the go-kart — from designing it to assembling the parts, with only help from the machine shop that offered welding support — was rewarding. I felt we went beyond merely having the knowledge, to understanding it.

However, my go-kart seemed unstable on fast turns, so I doubled my rear tires to help stabilize it. That meant I could go much faster around corners, but while I was testing my speed, on the fifth or sixth run my right front tire hit a rock and the kart flipped over, on top of me. My angle iron brake stopper cut into my ankle. I looked down and saw I was gushing blood, and knew I needed help.

A boy who lived next door to us saw me on the ground, ran over, and said he'd get my parents for me — but it was Saturday, and they were out running errands. So instead, he got his dad, Mr. Romero. I had never really talked to him, but he was incredibly ready to assist me.

Mr. Romero brought a bottle of red mercurochrome (for preventing infection) and a white towel to tightly cover the wound, but he could see that I had suffered a deep cut, so he decided to take me to the hospital. I still remember the soft-spoken and calm way he wrapped my wound and assisted me to the back seat of his car. At the hospital, a doctor cleaned the wound and stitched it closed. It only required 6 stitches, but the scar is still visible today. He then kindly drove me home and waited until my parents arrived.

This quiet man was like the extraordinarily kind Catholic priest in Japan that guided me to the hospital when I suffered my bicycle accident. In addition, I felt as though he was practicing my grandfather's teaching about life satisfaction emanating from serving others. Thus, I realized that I needed to embrace such understanding in my future years- continually thinking about others' needs and how I can assist them.

When we got tired of riding the go-carts, Mas thought of another engineering feat - modifying a bicycle into a homemade motorcycle. He designed and created a small engine that he had welded onto the bicycle's frame and linked with a chain to its sprocket. It had a homemade gas tank and straight dual pipes from the engine.

Mas's bike

As he drove down the parkway at 60 MPH, he caught the attention of a PA State police officer. He got fined for driving an unregistered and uninspected motor vehicle and was told that he couldn't drive the bike on public streets or highways. The officer kindly put the motorbike in his car's trunk — with the back tire sticking out — and brought Mas home. Luckily, I was the only one at home. Mas and I profusely thanked the officer.

Due to my sharing this event with some of my friends, Mas was now labeled as an ingenious kid. This event started to change his image from a "tough kid" to a "tough cool kid." I think this was a turning point. I felt that he was finally adapting to the US, somewhat shy of full acceptance. I believe one of the main reasons for Mas's unwillingness to leave Japan was due to his positive image and rewarding acceptance by his friends. At that time in Japan, he could not have imagined how foreign kids from the country that defeated Japan could offer genuine friendship and respect to him for being a unique and interesting person. He must have had much anxiety, fear, and bitterness over the possibility of rejection by his peers in the U.S. Thus, when his friends started to view him as positively unique and respectable, he no longer had to feel compromised or worthless. He was finding his niche and becoming more self-confident and composed. This transformation was slowly lifting my load of worries. I remembered promising my grandfather that I would be responsible and accountable for Mas's welfare and his contentment.

Senior year

After my junior year, the school changed the rules for electing class officers. Now, in the elections for class president and vice-president, they required a primary vote. If none of the candidates received 51% during the primary, the top two candidates would run against each other in the final round of voting.

I could read what seemed to be going on with this change — my IQ was, after all, at least 100 (despite my school record showing an IQ of 85). But this occurrence again reminded me of one of my grandfather's Words of Understanding:

If someone is more powerful than you — like a policeman, Father of the Catholic Church, the towns' mayor or the principal of a school, to name a few — never fight directly against him. Always remain polite and respectful, and then think of ways that you can go around him by contemplating and understanding why he is resisting you. If he is treating you unfairly, often it is also good to lose the battle and gain more respect from others who understand your predicament.

With this in mind, I politely refused the nomination for the senior class presidency — I understood that the school did not want me again as the class president — but instead accepted a nomination for vice-president. Many other students seemed to have also realized the reason behind the changed election rules. I overheard, for example, Pearl objecting to several students near her that this was an unfair change.

"They don't want Hide to win again," she said.

But I decided not to fight the school, because I knew it would be a fruitless battle, just as my grandfather had advised. And by choosing not to fight this battle, I gained significant amounts of empathy and kindness from my classmates. In my junior class presidential election, I won just 40% of the vote — but this time, when the results for the vice-presidential run were announced, I received over 60% of the vote. It seemed to me that I won a substantial number of sympathy votes from understanding students, some of which must have been also from the upper middle-class group.

My classmates were also amazingly cordial and kind to me in additional ways. Based on the end of year senior class survey, I was voted by my fellow students as among the guys:

The most artistic (#1);
Best physical figure (#1);
Excellent in clothes selection (#2);
Excellent dresser (#2); and
Most popular (#3.)

Soon after the SAT scores were available, my stepfather assisted us in applying to three schools: University of Pittsburgh, Duquesne University and Carrollton State College in Pennsylvania. He escorted us to meet the admissions directors to try to persuade them to admit us before they issued their rejection letters. Ultimately, both University of Pittsburgh and Duquesne University rejected our applications, and the admissions directors told us that our English SAT scores were too poor for us to survive through their courses. They also disliked our senior class grade point average of around 1.9, or a C-minus.

I secretly also applied to Carnegie Tech University — now known as Carnegie-Mellon University — because of their strong ranking in engineering. And without my stepfather knowing, I met with Carnegie Tech's director of admission. Remarkably, he indicated that due to my solid SAT score on math, I could have enrolled in a probationary status to see how I would do during the first semester's courses. He said that the school had a significant number of foreign students who weren't great at English — including some students from Japan — but said they all were able to complete the courses and graduate. He also noted that if I was more proficient in English, I might have scored well over 700 in SAT Math. The problem was that I wouldn't be able to receive any financial aid, and their tuition was about three times higher than local counterpart universities.

Because of this, my stepfather flatly rejected sending me to Carnegie-Mellon. So our last chance school was Carrollton State College (CSC) in Pennsylvania, which was located about 50 miles north of Pittsburgh.

After a lengthy meeting, the admissions director finally agreed to admit us, but he still expressed grave concern about our competence in English. Bill was ecstatic, because CSC's tuition was a mere $250 per year — much lower than the tuition at Pitt or Duquesne, which were each over $1,100.

In retrospect, I did experience a tough time trying to assimilate into and survive the academic rigor and challenges during my years at Eastwood High School. However, I believe my grandfather's lessons directly helped me to gain the friendship and confidence of my classmates. The Words of Understanding included the importance of earning the trust of the people around you, and how to avoid arrogance. It was also very helpful to know about his collection of beliefs that: "The scale of personal effort is an index of one's greatness," "A woman's beauty is her gracefulness," the importance of "good thoughts, good deeds, and companionship with good people," his declaration that "life satisfaction emanates from serving others, not through self-serving," and the distinction between knowledge and understanding- they are often unequal.

Even though I was far removed from

Japan, the lessons I learned during my early days in the Japanese school system also helped me at Eastwood High School, including the emphasis on developing good manners and good interpersonal relationships before knowledge. My lessons about the power and rewards stemming from collaboration among students were also helpful.

But my grandfather's worries about potential racial discrimination were largely unfounded. While some of the adults at school and community did treat us differently due to our Japanese descent, most of the kids treated us like any other student at the school. In fact, compared to the adults, I believe my grandfather would describe my white classmates as a collection of walking saints and angels — always fair to me and helpful when I needed their assistance.

Chapter 8

SUMMER STEEL MILL JOB: A LEARNING EXPERIENCE

AFTER MY GRADUATION from Eastwood High School, my stepfather arranged with the steel mill's hiring department for us to be employed as summer employees. The job paid $4.59 per hour, which was much higher than my previous summer job with a landscaping company that only paid $1.00 per hour. That job involved cutting the grass at a huge cemetery in the Southside (a group of neighborhoods across the Monongahela River from Downtown Pittsburgh). It took two of us seven days to complete. By the end of the seventh day, we needed to restart all over for another seven days. Mas worked at a gas station pumping gas for customers, sweeping, and cleaning tools. He was also paid $1.00 per hour. Thus, we were excited to begin working at the mill and potentially saving substantial amounts of money. But my stepfather warned us that our savings would go towards our college tuition, room and board, books, and other expenses. However, we would be able to buy a used car to commute to work. I immediately began to look for a used car.

After an extensive search, I found a great looking used car—a two-tone red and white 1956 Mercury Monterey. It was already eleven years old at the time, but the car had been kept in local storage for nearly seven years. It had shiny chrome bumpers and no visible dents or rust. Its interior looked like it had when it came off the assembly line. I got even more excited when I finally got the car started and its V8 engine rumbled to life. No cars sound better than those old 1950s V8 engines.

1956 Mercury Monterey

Mas was more interested in purchasing a motorcycle, and after several weeks he found and purchased a shiny black Yamaha that he adored. He used to ride it around with his friends, and he liked that so many girls were attracted to it.

Right after my purchase, I called Tom, who was well-known to be a great auto mechanic. He was knowledgeable about how to repair, modify, and replace engines. He also knew how to adjust brake shoes, modify the car's main springs, and install air shocks so it could take corners better. After much pleading, he came just about every weekend and on my day off from the steel mill to fix up my Monterey.

I managed to learn a lot about how to work on cars as I assisted him. I learned how to clean and reset carburetors, use a timing light and a dwell meter to adjust the engine's torque and horsepower, how to flush brake fluid, replace original mufflers with the glass-pack mufflers to improve the V8 sound and more. He also showed me how to dismount the V8 engine's volve covers and adjust its valve clearances. He had an old engine that had its crankshaft assembly removed and showed me how to look for damaged main bearings.

My savings from working at the steel mill allowed me to buy many of the tools needed for working on automobiles. I still use the hydraulic lifter that can raise an entire car about 3 feet off the ground and other smaller tools like a torque wrench and a socket wrench with a long handle. Tom was a quiet guy but an imaginative storyteller. He was a man with a good heart who would not hurt a fly—a genuinely decent and kind person. We became good friends hanging around tuning up and modifying my Monterey.

Tom's dad was a great talker as well. We used to sit around with him in the evenings as he lectured to us about American politics and the status of our economy while drinking his quart of beer. He was opinionated, to say the least. He said things like, "If I were the President, I would change this county within a year. I would put all of the crooked politicians right into federal prison." Tom and his family treated me as though I was their favorite adopted son. One day, Tom's dad hinted that he was thinking of moving the family to California. I remember asking him to please take me with them.

At the steel mill

My first day at the mill was unsettling. I was assigned to work at the hot mill, which had a line of enormous machines, well over twenty feet tall, that made huge noises as they hacked thick 8-foot-wide steel plates. There were giant, deafening cranes buzzing by on a rail mounted near the top of the tall ceilings, and piles of steel plates stacked over eight feet high. The mill was blisteringly hot during the summer; it reached 120 to even as high as 140 degrees depending on where you worked. To avoid fainting from extreme dehydration, all workers were required to carry a gallon jug of water and take salt pills as needed. Also, management strategically placed industrial fans that were about six feet in diameter to blast at workers so the heat would dissipate. Unfortunately, they simply swirled the hot air around.

The air was filled with flying dust and the floors were greasy. We had to yell directly into our coworkers' ears to be heard. Some were already losing their hearing from the constant cacophony. An alternative was to use hand signals, as long as the other worker knew that I was trying to communicate with them. There were quieter places in the mill, but most summer employees were placed in the harshest conditions, perhaps because the bosses believed that the young people ought to be able to take it and not complain.

As neophyte summer employees, we were assigned to the mill's worst jobs. Starting on my second day, I was sent to work in a long tunnel below the main floor where I had to shovel the scales into a big bin as the steel plates loudly rolled out of the furnace above. Then they were cooled with gushing water, which shed scales with the sound of a gazillion firecrackers going off at the same time. When the bin was shoveled full of scales, I would give a signal so a crane could remove it. The scale was hot, wet, and heavy. Inside the tunnel it was intolerably humid and dark, and even with my industrial mask on, I had to watch how I breathed in the heavy wet air. But I was not afraid of working like hell anywhere.

However, my third day at work a worker who had the job of removing the filled-up bins approached me angrily at lunchtime. He said, "If you slow down, you'll have your job tomorrow." He wanted to know why I was killing myself working so hard and wanted me to slow my pace. Apparently, he had to work harder too because I was filling up the scale bin too quickly, and he did not want to have to keep up with my tempo.

The following week, I was assigned to

another job. This time I was told to sweep the tool room and dispose of the dirt and trash into a garbage can. The foreman asked me to do it in eight hours. I was flabbergasted. Even working at a slow-as-a-turtle pace, I would only need about an hour to complete this job. Apparently, this was a punishment for my overdoing it during the previous week. I was bored to death, and it was a much more difficult day than working in that dark tunnel. For me, boredom is worse than an exhausting day of work. The eight hours seemed like twenty-four hours. I ended up complaining to my stepfather, and he said he would take care of it. He had some influence at the mill since he was an elected representative of the steel workers' union.

Then I was transferred again to the pipe mill section and assigned the job of separating the long rods (they looked like fluorescent red railroad rails) as they came out of the furnace. We had exactly seven seconds to separate the fused rods with an eight-foot steel pick. If you stayed longer than seven seconds, your fireproof light gray shirt, pants, and even eyebrows would start to smoke from the heat coming from the furnace, which melted iron at over 2,700-degrees Fahrenheit. Most of the permanent workers who worked that job had no eyebrows.

Eight of us, two guys at a time, rotated. We separated the long rods for seven seconds. Then we ran back to the seats beside the windows. Then we waited until our turn came up again—over and over. All day. Obviously, the heat during the summer months was almost unbearable. No fans were used in the vicinity of those furnaces because a stream of hot air could have instantly burned the workers. But I did not mind the job because the fast pace made the workday go by quickly.

After several weeks, I was again transferred to another location that was worse than the job at the pipe mill. It required working by a huge acid pit (about twenty feet in diameter and maybe fifteen feet deep) where a pile of steel plates would be washed clean of unwanted sediments marking the plates. One by one the plates were dipped into the acid pit to make the huge plates look spotless and shiny. I was told not to sit anywhere because the acid would eat holes in my pants.

My job was to guide the crane operator who lowered the steel plates into the acid pit. When it was clean and ready, I would signal him, and he would delicately pick them up until the remaining acid drained back into the pit. I used hand signals to tell him when to lower, shift from right or left, or stop or start picking up the steel plates. After each dip, the crane operator stopped working for about five to ten minutes. "Pacing the job for tomorrow," as he put it, while I stood waiting below. I learned by then to bring my own sheets of newspapers to sit on. As one may expect, it was challenging to breathe normally in the acid pit area. Plus, even with eye goggles, it was difficult to see because the fumes filled the entire area. Although it was unpleasant, I simply told myself to be patient, because I would likely be assigned to yet another job anyway.

Indeed, the following week I was assigned to work from midnight to eight a.m. in the cold mill. This job was easier than the previous jobs. I had to assist the steel sheet inspector by marking any imperfections on the steel sheets. All the imperfect steel sheets were separated from the good ones. This was a far less demanding job than my previous ones. My co-worker instructed me to assist him for about four hours and then disappear for a couple hours. He meant I should find a place to nap and use my watch to come back to work. So I found a relatively quiet closet where I would sit down and read a book or nap.

Summer employees were constantly assigned to jobs as needed when the permanent workers went on vacation. I realized that the steel mill workers were pacing themselves in hopes of avoiding potential future layoffs. Many of them seemed dissatisfied with their jobs. Not only did their job dissatisfaction decrease work performance and morale, but it may also have increased their motivation to support their union who fought the mill's administrators and "big shots" for wage increases. In part, such a work culture may also have contributed to Pittsburgh's steel mills shutting down during the subsequent years.

Gaining clarity on my life mission

For me, working in the steel mill was an immensely valuable experience. What I realized was that there was no way I wanted to be a steel mill worker or work in a similar occupation. All of these jobs were hellish, hostile, and boring. I realized more clearly that it would be far easier for me to study hard (even with the challenges associated with my language limitations) and focus on securing employment that demanded critical thinking rather than physical stamina and boredom management. I didn't want to be a young, burned-out full-time worker. Thus, focusing on my studies became one of my most important life missions. I feel blessed that my challenging time at the steel mill was able to provide this clarity.

However, I also gained tremendous respect for the steel mill workers who were burdened with a career they couldn't escape. They had little choice but to keep working in such strenuous conditions until old age. According to my stepfather, years before nearing 65, he and just about all the other middle-age steel mill workers dreamt about their retirement days.

Chapter 9

UNDERSTANDING MORE ABOUT MY STEPFATHER AND MOTHER

AFTER LIVING WITH my stepfather, Bill, and my mother for six years, and as my brother and I were getting ready to become college students, I began to understand more about my new parents.

Unfortunately, Bill was someone who thought he was always right and tended to dismiss the opinions of others. He rarely stopped talking and didn't give anyone else the chance to speak or interrupt him with questions. He seemed to suffer from some sort of superiority complex, and his behavior toward my mother was particularly telling. He judged her thoughts and feelings as wrong or less important. He often interrupted her and always had to have the last word.

He believed that he was smarter than my mother. She had a difficult time explaining her thoughts and logic because she emigrated to the US when she was an adult and therefore struggled with English. Sometimes he would shout, "You are so dumb; stop thinking, just listen!" He frequently corrected her word choices or mocked her by showing off that he had a better vocabulary. Once when she said, "I felt so sorry for Sophia (our neighbor's elderly wife) when her husband fell, and he ended up in the hospital."

He interjected, "You mean you felt empathetic," even though he knew that my mother did not know the meaning of that word. There was also an atmosphere of intimidation in our house. When she asked for money for household items like dry cleaning, he frequently responded with hostility. For example, he would respond to my mother, "When are you going to learn to manage your money? I already gave you $20 last week. You have no idea about the value of money that I earn working hard at the steel mill. Show some appreciation."

Scolding Mas

My mother wasn't the only one Bill directed his anger towards. Mas didn't care for our stepfather, and Bill knew how Mas felt about him. One night Bill demanded Mas make him a wooden paddle using his table saw in the basement. Every time Bill was unhappy with Mas's attitude, not listening or talking back, he ordered him to the basement and spanked Mas savagely with the board. Mas cried every time, begging him to stop. More than a dozen times I ran down to the basement and pleaded with him to stop. He couldn't care less about my pleading.

One night, Mas got so angry and dejected that he ran away from home in the dark. The next day, he told me that during the night police were patrolling the streets nearby, so he slid under a car to hide and sleep. But later he heard someone from the front porch telling his wife, "There is someone under our car, call the cops!" He slid out to the street side and ran home. No one except me realized that he was gone all night until he slid next to me in my bed with tears in his eyes, early the next morning. He simply could not stand our stepfather.

Bill was determined to "break him" like a wild horse needing to be humbled to respect a master. This type of physical abuse was very hard to take since our grandfather never hit us, not even once. When he was angry with us he would yell, but then he calmly talked to us so we would hear him and understand why he was angry and how to avoid making the same mistake.

Bill tended to focus on other people's flaws yet failed to notice his own. For example, he constantly criticized both his brothers for bad habits that he himself shared. He often ranted that his older brother was a cheapskate and a crook for not paying him interest on the $1,200 that he loaned him ten years earlier. When Bill complained about this, his younger brother pointed out that Bill had also paid no interest to their mother when she loaned him $1,000 for a down payment to purchase our house in Eastwood. According to Bill, his younger brother was a "dumb gambler" who was always losing money. However, Bill was an avid gambler who played cards with his steel mill buddies. They used to play every other week, some evenings at our house while my mother catered the gang's game with beer, chips, and sandwiches. We all knew when he lost his pot of $200 because he would irritably snap at our mother, creating tension until a few days before the next game.

He had no close friends. Except for his younger brother's visits on major holidays, there were no other social calls by anyone. His older brother never called or visited our house and was never invited to our house for dinner. Correspondingly, Bill never went with my mother to attend church social get-togethers.

He was also a cheapskate. On the rare occasion when we went on a vacation, he would make us walk from restaurant to restaurant so he could check the menu and its prices. Almost every meal was in a dingy, sketchy restaurant with horrible food. It was the same with motels. I learned to expect that the room would smell, the toilets would be filthy, and the beds uncomfortable because he refused to pay for anything but the cheapest place.

Also, he kept the burnt-out headlights and other internal bulbs to his old Ford Falcon. When it was time to make the trade, I had to help him switch them out with currently working old pairs. This was because he bought the same car model so he would be able to use the bulbs as needed sometime later. We also replaced the air filter with an old one and siphoned out windshield liquid and replaced it with water. He handed me a small flexible plastic tube to suck the liquid out until it began draining on its own into a container we laid out below.

He took great satisfaction in scamming others. His favorite stories were about swindling people because they were, as he saw it, so dumb. "Jewing them down," was a phrase that was tossed around when he mocked the people he took advantage of. As I noted, he felt that he was better than other people.

He also could be rude to others if it was safe to do so. When negotiating for his new car, he quoted a ridiculously low offer. When the salesman responded, "We would go broke with that kind of offer," he then took his hat off and started to walk around to other customers on the floor shouting, "Ladies and gentlemen, this dealer is going broke, please contribute to help them stay in business." The manager was so embarrassed he relented just to get him out of the dealership. He simply took pleasure in exploiting others to benefit himself and bragging about these stories over and over, as though he was trying to convince us that he was exceptionally smart.

Later in life, he seemed fine to Kathy and our children. He was calm, friendly, and funny. His behavior towards my mother was almost "gentlemanly," but that was only in front of others. When no one else was around, his behavior was often reprehensible.

Bill and Mother in Pittsburgh

One day my mother had to run out of the house barefoot in terror and hide in a neighbor's home because Bill was becoming violent, yelling about the dinner he disliked, throwing dishes at her, and upturning the dinner table. She called me from the neighbor's house to please come and get her.

I went to the police station and reported this event to the police chief before I brought her back to our home. Because she didn't have visible injuries, the chief indicated that he wouldn't bring Bill in, but if it happened again, he would arrest him.

After a few days in our house, my mother said she wanted to return home to take care of Bill. When we arrived I told him that I had reported the incident to the police. When I demanded an apology, he reluctantly said to my mother, "I'm sorry, I don't know what happened to me." Long before this incident, however, she had told me that there were frequent arguments between them, and he would be verbally abusive with her.

When Bill repeatedly had bad experiences with his steel mill coworkers, including an embarrassingly poor second election result, he decided at 53 years old to retire early from the steel mill, even with major penalties to his steel mill pension, and move my mother out of Pittsburgh. He decided, all on his own, that he and my mother would move to Las Vegas, and he would try surviving financially as a card-playing gambler. He sold their house in Eastwood, had a huge garage sale and packed everything they had left in their

Ford Falcon. As this event was unfolding, my mother called me crying and explained that we may not see each other for a long time. The decision had been made so quickly; she barely had any time to try negotiating with him.

I immediately went to see Bill and attempted to talk him out of the move. But he had already sent his boss a resignation letter. He had hired a realtor who already had found a potential buyer for their house. He'd done this without even hinting to me or his wife that he was thinking about moving. My mother seemed to reluctantly accept the fact that it was too late for her to try to change his mind, even though she wanted to stay close to her sons. Because of the cultural and parental influence on her to obey her husband, she swallowed her dislike and worry and went along with it. She wanted to make things as smooth as possible with her American husband.

Even though he played cards with mainly tourists as his potential prey, Bill did not financially survive as a gambler in Las Vegas. He also suffered several big losses during high stakes poker games that required an initial stake of $10,000 from every player. He did not earn enough and lost untold amounts of their savings they had from selling their house in Eastwood. In desperation, he ended up working as a gas station attendant and later as a gofer for a lock distribution company.

In their one-bedroom apartment, they did not have a telephone. Occasionally my mother and I exchanged letters, which repeatedly included her messages about how she was doing OK and not to worry about her. As often as I could, I visited them in their tiny apartment and slept on their beat-up, hand-me-down couch.

Understanding more about my mother

In the days of my mother's childhood, she and other Japanese women were taught to listen to their parents and obey them. Women were trained not to do things that might make others feel uncomfortable—to always consider the feelings of every person around them before their own. From an early age, my mother was told to accommodate rather than confront and to be obedient to Japanese male figures: father, husband, older brother, uncle, etc. She was taught to respect her husband and to attend to his needs first. Experiencing feelings of mutual love was a secondary concern.

Japanese culture in the 1940's and 50's also dictated that the wife is expected to stay home and take care of the household; cleaning the house almost every day was a typical routine of Japanese wives. Simultaneously playing the role of maid and loving mother, housewives were expected to do things like see their husband to the door with kind words as he departed for work. During those old days, Japanese husbands were typically intolerant and had selfishly "high" standards for their wives. They did not allow a wife to be headstrong. She had to exhibit good manners because husbands cared a lot about how others saw them. A wife appearing intelligent or insightful in front of men was discouraged.

Growing up with these strict cultural expectations trained her to rationalize Bill's intolerable treatment of her. When I reported Bill's abuse to the police chief, he asked me, "Why is she putting up with such abuse and mistreatment?"

My answer to him was, "Because she is a Japanese woman molded to accept submission and tolerate insults and exploitations." Thankfully, modern Japanese women are much more liberated after the WWII social influences of American and European cultures.

My mother was able to keep a smile when she was with other people. Even with her limited and heavily accented English, she tended to lighten the mood of a room and put everyone at ease. She chose to see the good in people instead of focusing on their flaws.

She was regretful about many things that happened in Japan after her arranged marriage to my father collapsed. She was impressed with my father because he had been an intelligent and brave navy pilot on an aircraft carrier. However, whether it was true or not, she thought that a communist owner of the newspaper tricked my father into writing the costly editorial. After my grandfather told her that she had to divorce, she fell into a deep depression, feeling a combination of confusion and despair that refused to go away. She went to church, often alone, to pray and ask for blessings so she wouldn't unravel.

To her, meeting Bill in Japan was a sign

that her obedient and complete devotion to God had been rewarded. At the beginning of their relationship, she didn't reveal to Bill that she was recently divorced and had two little boys, partially because she believed that no Japanese man would want her for these reasons—why would he? She assumed and hoped that eventually he would marry her. She had convinced herself that Bill could save her life, even though she had to reside in a foreign land 7,000 miles away.

As Mas got older, however, she sensed his regret about her previous inaction that had contributed to his placement in the dreadful orphanage. She regretted her decision but felt that in time Mas would forgive her since the past could not be changed. Out of fear of making things worse, she never expressed such sorrow directly to Mas. So they fell short of seeing eye-to-eye and continued to live on emotionally separate islands.

Chapter 10

COLLEGE LIFE AND MEET-ING SPECIAL PEOPLE

Y PARENTS MOVED Mas and I into our college dorm at Carrollton State College's (CSC's) campus on an early September Saturday in 1967. It was a bright, sunny day but unusually hot, well over 85 degrees. Luckily, we had relatively few items to move, just fall season clothes, camp size thermo-bottles, travel bag items, and our dictionaries. We were informed in the CSC's welcome letter that we could buy books and school supplies (notebooks, pens, color pencils, etc.) in the CSC's bookstore at a student discount.

Mas and I were placed on the first floor of a four-story concrete dormitory. The rectangular buildings were built perpendicular to each other. Each housed about 120 guys and had large communal bathrooms and showers in the center of each floor. Our room was only about 10 feet by 12 feet with one large window and walls made of sterile, white-painted cinder blocks. Mas and I each had a bed that was securely mounted to the floor on opposite sides of the room with a closet and desk right beside them.

We were not allowed to use nails or screws to hang our pictures and other items. So we simply used scotch tape to hang our favorite pictures of our grandparents (placed near my bed) and some rock groups like the Rolling Stones, Billy Stewart (who had just recently died of a car accident), and the Temptations. The building had no air conditioning, but we were told we were lucky to be on the first floor—first-floor rooms, with fans blowing, were always cooler than the higher floors, and the steam-driven heat system was sufficient for winter seasons.

On that first day we met the resident assistant (RA), who seemed too frail to oversee all the students on the floor. When we introduced ourselves, we explained that we came from Japan and were still learning English. One of the students asked, "Do you know Karate, Judo or Kendo?" We replied that we had some knowledge of all three.

The RA quickly responded, "Well, that

means no one will mess with you." One of the residents also asked us what our majors were—I said art. I had selected art because I had won art contests and I also suspected that the art department would not be so concerned about my SAT score in English, so I had a higher chance of being accepted into the program. Mas proudly said math. The RA told Mas that he'd heard they needed more math students and asked if he had gotten a scholarship. Mas, of course, told him no. All I could think about was that we were lucky to even be accepted for admission.

As my parents finally started to depart, my mother's parting words to me were, "Good luck, and make sure that Mas goes to every class and studies hard for the exams."

My stepfather added, "You hear that Mas?" At that instant I realized that the main reason behind their insistence that we go to the same college was for us to have each other as a source of emotional assurance and support and for me to watch over Mas, so he wouldn't flunk out. Such expectations corresponded with my grandfather's stipulation to me about being responsible for Mas.

My first term as a liberal arts student I had to take English, World Culture, and

Biology. And as an art major, I had to enroll in Art History and Introduction to Drawing. As may be expected, I got a D- on my first paper in English class. When I went to see the professor, his diagnosis was that while I have an ability to organize my ideas and thoughts on paper, my grammar was, at best, at a 6th-grade level. He suggested that before submitting my final term paper, I should rely on an English major or even consider getting outside help to proofread and edit my papers. Since we were considered foreign students, he said that would be fine with him. I told Mas about our meeting, and from that point on we did secure immensely helpful support from students majoring in English literature.

I soon realized that majoring in art was a big mistake. First, my fellow art majors were much more talented than I was. In addition, the art classes were mostly boring and difficult, especially the class on art history that included lengthy reviews of Renaissance art, the Baroque period, and modern art. Besides, the instructor kept warning us in his lectures, "You are here to learn how to enhance your creativity, not to make lots of money." That didn't make me feel very reassured about my prospects. He wanted mission-driven, not paycheck-driven, art students.

Just before my second semester, I met with my academic advisor and changed my major to Economics, so I hadn't really wasted any credits. Unfortunately, I also found economic classes boring—they demanded not just math skills, which I had, but we also had to read and try to understand dry economic theories. This was tiresome because I did not find such topics to be captivating.

However, I will never forget one professor who taught Introduction to Economics. Dr. Taylor was in his late 70s. When he was a young banker, he had become a millionaire by investing in the right combination of stocks. He was so well-off that when the college needed a new chemistry building, he financed a substantial portion of the cost as a charitable donation to the institution.

He was an interesting and engaging lecturer, but what he did at the end of the term was exceptionally unusual and has stuck with me ever since. Right after taking his final exam, Dr. Taylor told us all to line up in the hallway outside his classroom and come in to speak to him, one by one. Out of twenty or so students, I was in the middle of the pack, and one of my friends, Porter, was about three or four students behind me. As I went into the room, Dr. Taylor was already smiling.

His kind demeanor reminded me of my grandfather, which made me comfortable and somewhat relaxed. He first asked how I liked his class. I told him that although my exam scores were relatively low—typically Cs—that I had learned a lot from his lectures. After a few other questions, he finally asked, "Well, then what do you think you earned in this class?" I reluctantly said, "An A?" I figured I had nothing to lose. He took a few seconds and whispered, "Alright. But don't tell anybody." My friend Porter was honest, and told him he felt he deserved a C. So I got an A, and Porter got a C for our final grade. I believe such an event would never occur in Japan!

I think about Dr. Taylor even today. What I understood much later in life was that an exam is a necessary tool for learning, but it does not necessarily represent the individual's ability to capitalize on the information he's been taught. Thus, by itself, an exam score may misrepresent what is invaluable in life: the ability to go beyond knowledge to understanding and to incorporate that knowledge for a useful purpose. According to my grandfather, knowledge does not guarantee understanding. For example, an individual may know impressive amounts of trivia (e.g., names of all the Oscar award winners since 1929), but they may show no capacity to apply it for useful purposes, like writing an article or column about how and why winners' selection criteria has changed over the years for others to learn and appreciate.

So, I think Dr. Taylor wanted to remain humble when judging his students based solely on knowledge-based exam scores. But I have no idea what he saw in me that he felt OK to give me a much higher grade. However, I will always fondly remember him. I am certain that he had no idea and never expected that he would be adored and appreciated, even long after his passing, perhaps by many of his other students as well.

By sophomore year I switched my major to Psychology, and that's where I landed for good. I felt at home going to the psych classes, studying for the exams, and writing term papers. The lectures were much more interesting. I also felt good about studying how to help people who suffered from anxiety and depression due to their hostile life events and unbearable circumstances. And I thought that such a profession would certainly have made my grandfather feel proud and gratified.

The psychology course I liked most was Experimental Psychology, which required heavy doses of statistics and math-based logical deduction. To my surprise, after the midterms my professor asked me in front of the class if I would mind helping students who were having difficulties with the statistical calculations. I said I would be honored to provide my assistance. Right after that class, six students waited for me to make an arrangement to meet.

Foreign language requirement

During my sophomore year, we were informed that all liberal arts students were required to take courses in a foreign language. Instead of struggling with yet another language, the way I did with French in high school, I proposed to our advisor that he consider counting our knowledge of Japanese, our native language, as fulfilling the language requirement.

He agreed but said that as a formality he needed proof that we actually knew Japanese. Thus, he suggested that he would contact a friend of his who was a Japanese professor at the University of Pittsburgh and ask him to test us to confirm our language proficiency. Mas and I were both pleased by this plan.

A few weeks later we met his friend, Dr. Miller. We spoke in Japanese about campus life at CSC and how we were adjusting to American culture. After our session, he had no doubts about our ability to speak Japanese and assured us that he would send a letter of confirmation to our advisor. That was a huge relief because it saved us considerable time and from the difficulty of learning a third language.

College social life

All the students who lived on campus resided in dormitories or fraternity and sorority houses. Campus residents ate at a super huge cafeteria-style dining room that was the size of a gymnasium. There must have been 30 or more dining tables each with seating for eight to share the evening's meal. There were no assigned seats at the tables.

Despite hit or miss meals, it was a perfect way to socialize. We'd just line up in a hallway to meet whomever and dine together, which gave us a great opportunity to meet other students—especially attractive girls.

I used to go with Mas to line up, and if we saw a pretty girl, we simply moved to line up for her table. So, we both saw and met several great looking college girls. One of the first girls I met was named Millie, who seemed shy but had a very pretty face. When I saw her at the first dance for new students, with nearly 1,000 attendees. I asked her if she would dance with me. She agreed, and we danced mainly slow dances. I was grateful that Deli had taught me well during my high school days. We quickly became friends and met often to attend school events together, like students' art shows and basketball games, and to some fraternity parties as well. Many might have thought that we were going steady, but we had no such commitment.

Meeting Kathy

Meanwhile, my brother Mas was dating a high school sophomore named Melissa that he met in Pittsburgh during the previous

Christmas holidays. Her school, East Catholic High, was having a dance event— the Sophomore Hop—and she asked him to be her date. She also asked him if I might be interested in taking her best friend Kathy to the dance. When Mas mentioned this to me, I said, "Sure, why not." I thought Mas wanted me to accompany him so he could be more at ease with his date, as well as people at the dance. But immediately I became somewhat uneasy because I was already a sophomore in college. Kathy was a high school sophomore, and I didn't know anything about her. I asked Mas if Kathy was pretty or not, but he had no idea because he hadn't met her yet. Thus, it was essentially a blind date.

When the day came for me to meet her parents and sister before escorting her to the dance, it was a unique experience. I was instantly drawn to Kathy's beauty. She was dazzling, with a porcelain complexion, hazel green eyes and fiery red hair held back with a colorful barrette. She wore an all-white dress that made her look, to me, angelic. Although she was only a sophomore in high school, she seemed both self-assured and humbly reserved.

Her mother's demeanor was noticeably

controlled but accommodating as she led me to their living room. It was well decorated with a new couch, comfortable-looking chairs, an artistically crafted dark coffee table, and a painting from the Renaissance period that had a humanistic, Christian reflection. But I immediately sensed her father's uneasiness. Although he barely looked directly at me, he abruptly interrogated me.

He surprised me with brusque questions like, "When did you immigrate to this country?" "What does your father do?", and "Where do you live in Eastwood?" The questions went on and on, making me nervous. Kathy's sister was silent, but she offered reassuring smiles from time to time. Kathy looked as though she was as nervous as I was, frequently glancing at her mother to intervene as her dad persisted. As we walked to the car she was somewhat apologetic and said, I just want you to know that my dad does that to everybody. And I think my mother and sister liked meeting you.

The dance went very well. Kathy seemed composed and enjoyed slow dance music. She repeatedly said, "I love this song," to tunes like "High on a Hill" by Scott English, "Forever" by The Marvelettes, and "Unforgettable" by Nat King Cole. A number of Kathy's friends came by, seemingly to check me out. I gathered that some could not believe that she brought a college student to her dance, let alone a Japanese person. Others were very friendly and said things like, "I would like to visit Japan someday," "I love Japanese Honda motorcycles," or "My dad loves Japanese cameras—like Nikons." After the dance, as I was walking up the steps with her to her door to say goodbye, I told her that I had a wonderful time, and I would like to keep in touch—maybe through letters or notes until my return during the summer months.

As soon as the CSC Spring semester ended for the summer break, I called to ask Kathy if she wanted to go to a movie with me. Without hesitation, she said yes but warned me that she first had to check with her parents. She did manage to get her parents' OK and so we went to a local theater to see West Side Story.

That evening I was convinced that she was a special person, and I wanted her to be my eventual girlfriend. For being such a young woman, she seemed so self-assured and graceful—the trait my grandfather had taught me was the best-kept secret of beauty. During our date, I told her that one of my hobbies was photography, even though I could not afford to purchase great cameras. I asked if I could take some photos of her the following weekend. She agreed.

She called me later and told me to pick her up after dinner at a drugstore near her house. I gathered that maybe she hadn't gotten her parents' permission to go out. That was OK with me, but I was concerned that she may face punishment from her dad and that he would say she could never date me.

On that day, I gathered my camera, flash, film, and a blanket and went to pick her up. She was in a perfectly-fitting summer dress with a green design—which I later found out she actually had made—she looked like a beautiful magazine model. We drove to a nearby park, and I noticed how she seemed so relaxed and comfortable. I was nervous that my photos might not do her appearance justice. I worried that I couldn't fully capture her exceptional loveliness and attractiveness. Doing my best, I took several photos of her using a flash as sundown started to take over. Because she alerted me that she didn't want to be out too late, I gathered my things and promptly drove her home. When I saw my photo of her, I was elated.

My photograph of Kathy

Not only had I captured her beauty but also it was an artistic depiction of her curvaceous posture, the stylishness of her beautiful red hair neatly tied back, and the elegance of her face, like a beautiful half-moon. Such a photo would never have been possible if she had felt awkward—she was calm, assured, and stress-free at that very moment. This realization further inspired my attraction towards her. I definitely wanted her to get to know me as a unique and good person.

I found out later, however, that when her father saw this photo, he was very upset that she didn't ask for his permission for this photo session. He was angry that the picture showed that it was taken in the dark and she was sitting on the blanket looking "suggestive."

Because her father was strict, dating Kathy was a challenge. She had to carefully check in with her parents before going out with me, and their answer would depend on her dad's constantly changing mood. I never received a welcoming greeting from her father. And it was disheartening to be greeted by him looking very unhappy as I came to pick her up for a date.

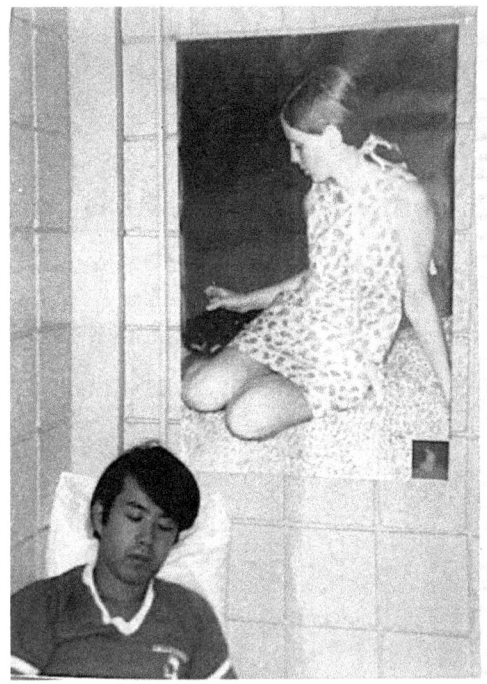
Kathy's photo in my dorm room

Despite such challenges, I got to know Kathy more during the summer. I found her to be a kind, nurturing, highly intuitive, and an emotionally intelligent person. This was clear in our first deep discussion after seeing the movie West Side Story, which was a musical about the rivalry between two teenage street gangs of different ethnic backgrounds. She felt that the movie's themes of love striving to rise above group-based hatred, the unjustifiable fear of immigrants, and the injuriousness of racism and bigotry made it particularly meaningful. She told me that our society tends to be confused about the essence of love and happiness, which can be shared between anyone who is caring and good to each other.

Her perceptive observations made me feel that she was a remarkably special individual. Thanks to my grandfather's teaching, I understood and very much appreciated her insights. Although it was early in our relationship, I was convinced at that moment that Kathy was the right person for me, but I feared that I might not be good enough for her. Because she was so pretty, I also knew that many other guys would pursue her—perhaps even with her dad's blessing. Fortunately, we continued to build our fondness for each other in the coming years.

Pledging and Joining a Fraternity

During the fall term of my sophomore year, the fraternities on campus recruited new members. I wanted to join a fraternity because during the weekends, campus town was essentially dead. There were virtually no fun activities. Most non-fraternity students just sat in bars and drank heavily, and the campus girls stayed away from heavy drinkers. Meanwhile, fraternities had huge weekend parties, in some cases as many as 200 people were invited by the brothers. Thus, if you wanted to meet people and have an enjoyable social life, it was a smart choice to join a fraternity.

Fortunately, some of the fraternity recruiters invited me to meet other fraternity brothers during their evening parties and social events. After meeting three fraternities, I was convinced that Alpha Lambda Chi (ALC) was the best choice for me. The other two fraternities seemed slightly uncomfortable with me being a racial minority. I could sense how some fraternity brothers were acting and reacting to my presence. I felt that the overall interpersonal IQs of the other two fraternities were below an acceptable level. It was obvious to me that they hesitated to introduce me to the girls attending the parties. Too much of my time at those fraternity socials was like going to a new unfriendly bar. I had to start the conversations with brothers whom I had never met before, instead of being treated as a guest that got to be introduced to everyone. It's their silence that signaled their uneasiness with my attendance.

The ALC, on the other hand, already had a Black brother, and they showed no hesitation in introducing me to everyone as though I was their old friend. So I decided to pledge to the ALC fraternity.

We had a pledge group of 24 individuals for the fall term. Because we had to do whatever the brothers demanded, the pledging period was quite an experience. By the way, the hazing that I describe was discontinued right after our pledge season at CSC.

I hated the hazing experience, especially because of my teachings in Japan that emphasized respect for others, as well as the lessons my grandfather taught me about dignity, compassion, and responsible behavior. But I thought I had to emulate and act like a young American college kid. I was, after all, in the US, not Japan. So I was determined to stick it out and finish pledging. I did not want to be a quitter.

The very first week, three of us were directed to go to the University of Pittsburgh's girl's dorm and bring back unwashed panties from three specific girls that some of the brothers had known during their high school days. When we made our request, not surprisingly, all three girls initially refused because we wouldn't tell them who issued the request. We persisted and I told them that we would be punished if all three panties were not secured. When nothing worked, I offered to pay $10 per panty. Finally, one of the girls offered to give us three pairs of her own underwear for $30 but warned us that two of them had holes. We said no problem—we figured the guys wouldn't know the difference! We thanked her and left feeling that our first mission was successfully accomplished. We put the panties into three envelopes with the names of each girl, and the brothers were pleased that we completed our mission.

Another pretty outlandish prank was already a well-known ritual at CSC. We had to attach a long string with a pen at the end to our Mr. Happy. Then, using this pen, we had to collect 30 signatures from girls on campus. Many girls, knowing full well where the string was tied, still readily used the pen to sign.

I felt there was no way to get out of these initiation rituals, so I was ready to put up with it all. I become comfortable with feeling uncomfortable when I experience intolerance from time to time in my life. Thus, I was ready to rationalize the experience, better than other pledges that seemed to dread it much more than I did. I also thought about how my father must have endured his training and initiation as a navy pilot on the aircraft carrier. I was sure that he had much more horrifying days than my pledging experience.

However, by the day before Hell Night, 14 pledges had quit. They decided that joining the fraternity was not worth suffering through the despicable rituals. Only 10 of us remained as "obedient" pledges.

Hell night

The hazing rituals all culminated in "hell night," which was supposed to be our final test before we could join the fraternity. We had to eat specially prepared, disgusting mud-like food, drink awful smelling and tasting drinks (they called it "nectar of the gods"), and participate in undignified games, to say the least. For example, in one game we were required to pick up an olive that was placed on an upside-down whisky cup with our butt cheeks and deliver it to another cup about 10 feet away. If we dropped the olive, we had to eat it. We also had to line up and take apart the guts of a recently shot rabbit and smear it on our faces. I remember even today that the rabbit was still lukewarm. Moreover, we had to wear burlap sack underwear, which was intended to be extremely itchy, but Kathy kindly lined mine with silk cloth, so it felt bearable. I also tucked a $20 bill into the lining of the underwear just in case.

At around midnight, we were blindfolded, thrown into the backseat of one of the brother's cars, and taken for a ride. I was in a car with two other pledges, Phil and Steve. We had no idea where we were going because we couldn't see anything at all. They drove for about two hours until they dropped us off at a frozen lake. We were told to stand there on the frozen ice facing away from the shore and count to 50 before taking off our blindfolds. By the time I got to about 12, Phil shouted: "Stop counting, Hide, they are gone." Being raised in Japan, I was simply used to following an instruction to its full extent.

When I took off my blindfold, all I saw was the bright moon above and an iced-over lake surrounded by wide-open fields. There were no markers indicating our location, no homes or buildings anywhere. Steve wondered, "Any idea where we are?" We had no clue because they took so many turns along the way we couldn't get our bearings. I noted that we could be in any number of states—Pennsylvania, West Virginia, Ohio, or even Maryland. I suggested we just start walking and look for road signs.

We walked for 30 minutes or so, seeing only barren dirt roads and farmland with no homes, street signs, or markers. Finally, we stumbled upon a farmhouse with lights on. Phil suggested that we ask whoever lived there where we were. It must've been three a.m., but we were desperate, so we knocked on the door several times and waited. Finally, an old man appeared.

Phil asked, "Could you tell us what state we are in?"

We must've looked awful—I'm sure our faces were still stained with the rabbit's blood—I didn't blame the old man for immediately slamming the door shut. But still, we were stranded, with no idea where we were. And we were cold because we were under-dressed for the icy weather. We decided to just keep walking.

After what seemed like forever, we started walking towards the sounds of 18-wheelers and eventually found a two-lane highway. Soon, we saw a sign that designated the road as Route 43S and another nearby sign that said, "Cheat Lake 5 miles." We were in West Virginia, and Phil knew that we needed to head north for about 60 miles to reach our campus.

Finally, after another half-hour or so of walking in the cold, we saw a small roadside diner that looked open, even though it must've been nearly five a.m. by that point. We immediately dashed to the men's room and washed our faces. We were lucky that I had packed that $20 bill—we were able to order something to eat. Using the diner's public payphone, Steve called his dad to come and get us. We were back at our fraternity house by 8:00 a.m. We were the first among the three pledge groups to return.

Meeting my lifetime college friends

After sharing various activities as pledges and as fraternity brothers, I met three special ALC members: Phil, Emil, and Stan. They became my life-long friends. Overall, as I got to know them, I felt that they liked me just as I am, so there was no need for me to be pretentious to please them. They understood me, and I understood them, and they appreciated my presence in their lives. I felt their approval and camaraderie as they introduced me with tones of fondness to their friends and girlfriends, including to super good-looking female guests at our fraternity parties and campus activities. I noticed that I was frequently included in their conversations with others. For example, they would say: "Hide is from Japan, and he is an artist," or "If you want to hear a collection of fine music, visit his room and have him turn on his great sound system." Often it was as though they were bragging about what I was like to others who did not yet know me.

I also felt that I could openly share my thoughts and beliefs even if they were contrary to their perspectives or unfamiliar to them. For instance, all three favored further strengthening the US military, but I disagreed. I felt free to tell them what I thought about US arms buildup: "If you are for arms buildup, you are for killing more innocent people—children, women, and the elderly—than all the soldiers combined. Just look at WWII statistics." Or that I felt that, "Black women are mostly ignored by the media. There should be many more movies and commercials including their presence."

Their natural response was to actively listen to me, which made me feel free to be open about my thoughts and perceptions. And I felt secure and protected about unveiling my personal and individual opinions. For instance, I felt free to share that I wished I had a chance to get to know and kiss a Japanese girl, but I never dated or met a Japanese girl my age. Stan, in response, said, "I bet they feel the same as anyone else, if you adore her." I believe good friendship must include such active listeners who are eager to engage with each other's thoughts. Even when we disagreed, we often intellectualized it and communicated with each other in a tone of mutual respect and appreciation for the other person's feelings. We understood that there were two sides (or more) to any argument or perspective.

We also shared many similar interests, especially regarding pop music (e.g., The Mamas & The Papas, The Beatles, Righteous Brothers, Little Anthony, The Box Tops, Procol Harum, Rolling Stone, Santana, just to name a few). We also appreciated great sports cars (e.g., Corvettes, Shelby Cobra, Ford GT40, Mustangs, including European contenders like Ferrari, Lamborghini, and

Porsche.) All of us were fond of outdoor activities and spent countless hours camping, canoeing, fishing, and hiking together. Like many others, we also liked sports (e.g., football, especially the Steelers, college basketball, baseball, the Kentucky Derby, etc.) And all three of us had affable, socially attentive, and great-looking girlfriends, who further strengthened our bond with each other, especially because our girlfriends liked being together. However, the three individuals were uniquely different from each other as well.

Phil

As we pledged together, I found Phil to be an interesting conversationalist. We also shared similar interests—like travel and pretty girls—as well as similar beliefs about the importance of hard work and honesty. He was serious and thoughtful but lighthearted and funny, and he said things like, "If you can't earn your keep, you are a worthless person," or, "One day I would like to visit and travel throughout Japan and meet all the good-looking girls, I mean people."

He approached life with a glass half-full

optimism and had an ability to always look on the bright side in nearly any situation. For example, he would say to me "I know you got a C on this exam, but knowing you, you'll get an A on the next one." His mind seemed to be constantly working, even when we were just quietly hanging out. He thrived on social interactions and had no problem making friends with both guys and girls. He was also a good listener, who asked good questions, and knew how to keep a conversation going for hours on end without it becoming boring.

I still remember well how he used to invite me to lunch at his home, about 10 miles off campus. His mother (an aunt who adopted him) would always be waiting with a hot meal, and she was a fantastic cook. She would make everything from meatballs, kielbasa, and hot sausage sandwiches to homemade vegetable and chicken noodle soups, and a variety of cookies and delicious apple pies.

By my second year, I had bought a Honda motorcycle and brought it to campus. I modified it with a tall steering wheel—to make it like a Hell's Angels bike. The bike didn't have a muffler, just loud straight chrome pipes. We used to ride the bike to

Phil's house looking cool with him wearing the WWII Defense Force's Helmet on his head.

I enjoyed visiting Phil's home because his uncle and aunt who raised him were decent and kind. I sensed such feelings as we talked with a wonderful level of mutual respect, interest, and engagement. It was very clear to me that they also liked my friendship with Phil. So as time went by, Phil became my best friend, and we hung out all the time at the fraternity house and restaurants and bars near campus and attended many campus events.

As I got to know him more and more, Phil stood out as an exceptional individual. He was honest, polite, and generous with compliments to others. He always seemed to be thinking of others, and easily shared his belongings, including his beautiful metallic green 1966 Mustang. When he found out that Kathy was coming to see me, he would say, "Hide, here is the key for my Mustang. Take her to a good restaurant." We both enjoyed sipping cold beer on the weekends and at social get-togethers. He often dated affable and great girls, whom I got to know as well.

My Honda and me with a bicycle hand bar

He was also an adventurer, seeking to balance an intense life of social relationships, travel, and exploration with plenty of downtime to relax and enjoy the moment. If it were up to him, he would spend his life exploring the world from one country to another. In fact, right after his graduation, he and another ALC fraternity brother nicknamed Pha-Pha decided to go to Australia to see if they could find a job and live in Sydney, Melbourne, or Brisbane. They didn't know anybody in Australia to guide them, but felt that since they spoke English, they would be able to get around without serious problems.

Well, after 2 years, Pha-Pha met a girl whom he wanted to be his future wife, and since Phil hadn't found a good-paying job, he flew back to the US and worked on an Alaskan pipeline for a while before returning to his hometown. Later he worked as a federal mine inspector and retired comfortably with his wife who was an exceptional art teacher. We still get in touch via phone at least four to five times a week.

Emil

Another brother I got to know well was Emil, who was my roommate at the fraternity house. He was the captain of the CSC college football team and president of his class and our fraternity. Obviously, he was in great physical shape as a star football player at our college, and his team was named 40 years later to the Hall of Fame. But he also was extremely intuitive and emotionally in-tune with other people. He was a bundle of energy, had lots of charm and charisma, and he could easily get things going by leading people along. For example, when our fraternity house was scheduled to be inspected by the dean of students (to make sure the house was safe, no guns or drugs, etc.), he already had sheets with the list of who was to do the cleaning and inspection and by when. He also had assigned a specific person to double-check the original person's duties. Such organized leadership made our tasks efficient and effective.

He was unusually good at conceptualizing ideas and opportunities that others did not see as well. He was open-hearted, generous, and big-spirited—a natural social light. As president of our fraternity, I saw how he refrained from strong-arming or using coercion, but rather he relied on his communication skills to help the brothers see another side to an issue or problem. Because he was able to see various points of view and grasp the big picture, he naturally excelled at crafting compromises and efficiently achieving mediation between groups having a disagreement. For example, issues related to the fraternity budget for different needs were efficiently resolved because of the talent he exhibited. He skillfully resolved the issues like fixing front steps vs. replacing outdated sound systems vs. building a new outdoor bar. He simply prioritized the list based on the seriousness of need vs. want.

Back in college as today, Emil was fiercely attracted to intelligence and creativity. He adored stories about insights and smart ideas to solve problems. He was also unafraid to roll up his sleeves and get to work and wouldn't blink an eye at laboring overtime to get the job done. He operated as though he would never run out of energy. When his goal was set, it got done—despite any obstacles that came up.

Like Phil, he was also a good listener who could further expand upon someone else's thoughts. Such abilities made others feel that he was a trustworthy person; someone who was highly capable and appreciative of accurately comprehending another's point of view. Like what my grandfather taught me, he knew, even as a young college student, that the most important trait of leadership is gaining the trust of others.

Emil wisely invested in a start-up chemical company and became one of three owners. When Emil and his partners sold the chemical business, he had already achieved his career goal of financial independence and was able to retire early at age 60 and travel around the world.

Stan

My third great friend was Stan. He recently passed away after suffering from a relentless cancer. Stan's strength and stamina were clearly illustrated by how he endured his grueling health journey with amazing willpower and noble spirit.

During our college days, Stan, like many of us, was trying to figure out how to secure a good future life. As a young man, however, he was already intuitive about the meaning of life and often invited deep discussions with people from various perspectives. Stan also stood out because he was great at anything physical. In boxing, no one could beat him; no one could rebound better than him in basketball; and no one could even dance as well.

Stan was another natural group leader like Emil, but he had strict rules about what was right and wrong and how we should treat each other in order to create lifelong friendships. He was a succinct communicator and avoided mincing words or practicing "politically correct" language. After Emil's presidency, Stan was elected and became the much-adored president of our fraternity.

My friends - Stan, me, Emil, and Phil

Stan also appreciated a variety of life-concepts such as the complexity of nature (e.g., how the universe affects earth), variety of artistic vision (e.g., culturally unique artwork), quality music (e.g., Mozart - Requiem in D minor KV 626 - H. von Karajan - Berlin Philharmonic Orchestra), and creativity (e.g., new ideas such as Amazon). He was also guided by key principles; for example, the value of logic and deductive reasoning, spiritual strength and power, mission-driven actions, and the merits of love and kindness. But most of all, he adored his beautiful girlfriend and later his wife, Thea, and his wonderful children and grandchildren who completed his successful life of affluence, gratitude, and enlightenment.

I still remember Stan having potato

chips and vitamin pills as his main dinner in college—that's all he could afford at that time. But his temporary poverty had no impact on him or his career. He retired as a vice president of a nationally known company, La-Z-Boy USA.

For over 50 years, all four of us have kept up a close friendship since the days we lived in the ALC fraternity house. We kept regularly communicating and meeting several times a year to enjoy the summer and winter season with our wives who got along exceptionally well. More about our friendship is included in the final chapter.

Mas and Bunny

During our sophomore year, Mas came to me and told me, "I finally met a girl that I really like. Her name is Yvonne, but her nickname is Bunny." She was one academic year ahead of Mas and majoring in elementary education with a minor in French. They dated most of Mas's sophomore and junior years. They finally decided to get married during his senior year before his college graduation. As I got to know Bunny, I told Mas that she was the best thing that ever happened to him.

With a lively and creative spirit, Bunny is always optimistic and full of energy, which makes her a joy to be around. She aims to create an environment around her that is bountiful with love and comfort. She is extremely caring and giving towards those she loves. Although she is gifted with great intelligence, she remains humble—the kind of person who knows how to listen and genuinely wants to understand you. With her non-judgmental nature and an upbeat cheerfulness, she easily invites close friendships.

Bunny is reliable and honest but not a gullible person, and she will not easily change what she believes in. Others do not easily influence her. She doesn't mind waiting in long lines, or when her food takes a long time at the restaurant. Bunny is very aware that anything worth getting takes time. She possesses a calm and gentle nature and doesn't get upset easily.

Bunny will also do anything within her power to ensure that the ones she is closest to are looked after well, and she takes great pride in taking care of people. Again, Bunny is by far the best woman for Mas. His life has been gifted with numerous blessings because this wonderful, dedicated person as his wife and wonderful mother of their children.

Bunny told me, "I liked that Mas was such an honest and kind young man with no pretenses." She was fascinated by his Japanese culture and thought that he was a handsome young man. She also said, "My dad, who passed away when I was 9 years old, came to me in a dream and told me, 'Bunny, he's a good man.'"

Mas mentioned to me, frequently, how he hit it off well with Bunny's mother, Nonna. She always cooked great meals for him, and she supported him on any and all issues, like when there was a disagreement about how the basement should be remodeled, what kind of roses should be planted in his front walk, or where to vacation next summer. Mas's suggestions were the ones that Nonna supported. That's something he never received from our mother or stepfather.

He also got along great with Bunny's brother-in-law, Les, who was an electrical engineer and shared Mas's interest in math and physics. He also got along well with Les' kids: Lili, Nina, and Barry. Bunny's sister Vee and brother Mondo were also delightful and treated Mas as though he was their dear brother. Mas never had any problem with Bunny's family or friends. In 1978, Mas and Bunny took Nonna into their home to live with them as she got older and found it difficult to live by herself. Mas and Bunny took her everywhere including shopping trips, dinners, holiday get-togethers, and on family vacations. She lived with Mas and Bunny together very well for 22 years until her passing.

I never understood why, but our mother disliked Bunny. According to Mas, our mother lied to Mas about Bunny's love letters that she sent to him during our college days. When Mas discovered that our mother threw away several of Bunny's letters, she told him that soon she and he would go to Japan and look for a Japanese wife. Perhaps she did this because she knew how badly Mas had wanted to go back to Japan. But out of courtesy, Bunny sent wedding invitations to Bill and our mother, but Bunny never received their reply. So at the wedding, Bunny and Mas were shocked when they saw them sitting at the table slated for others.

Thus, my college years were filled with blessings. Meeting some unique professors. Unforgettable experiences associated with pledging. Meeting and appreciating lifelong friends, and my completion of the liberal arts degree program in Psychology.

During those years I used to get on my Honda motorcycle and drive to Kathy's dorm on the weekends. Other weekends she came to see me at CSC, and we dated like any other couple in love, going out to restaurants, fraternity parties, football games and CSC dance events. Everyone knew that we were a committed couple going steady and enjoying each other's company.

With relatively low grades during my freshman and sophomore years, I needed to raise my overall grade point average (GPA) because I wanted to continue my education. I also thought about working more directly with communities instead of clinically focused work with afflicted individuals one-on-one. Thus, the next chapter describes my personal transformation through my post-graduate studies, including unanticipated challenges and events.

Chapter 11

GRADUATE SCHOOL AND DOCTORAL PROGRAM

D URING MY SENIOR year of college, I decided to continue my education and earn a master's degree. As noted, this decision stemmed directly from my steel mill work experience. I realized then that it would be far easier to study hard and secure a position which would require that I use my brain than to end up in a job that relied on my physical stamina. As I was completing my major in Psychology, I also felt that I wanted to work more directly with people in need. As I saw it, clinical psychology was focused only on individuals and not at all on addressing broader societal problems like poverty and child abuse. Other major categories of psychology, like cognitive and behavioral psychology, were too theoretical or medically oriented for my comfort.

I thought I might want to pursue a master's degree in social work. Kathy and I had continued to date throughout college, so I went to her to discuss this decision. She was supportive and reassuring; she said that our society needed social work services in several areas. She felt that the US, as the richest nation in the world, should not have such an array of social problems. Growing up in Johnstown, Pennsylvania, a working-class steel town east of Pittsburgh, she'd seen how poverty could impact parents and their young children and that chronic unemployment could often lead to destructive alcohol and drug addiction.

I also thought that social work encompassed what my grandparents admired about their own three daughters, who became Catholic nuns in the Charity order. They focused on community initiatives to benefit sick, marginalized people, and destitute families and children. They devoted themselves to a life of spiritual perfection and service to needy people through God's blessings. Social work also aligned well with one of my grandfather's "Words of Understanding": satisfaction with life comes from serving others, not through serving oneself, and that the reward of enlightenment accompanies compassion and generosity to others.

However, I needed to know more about what kind of career I could have with social work, so I wrote to the Dean of the School of Social Work at the University of Pittsburgh, Dr. David Epperson. I asked to meet with him to discuss what makes social work so unique and special. He responded immediately, offering to meet with me in his office any Thursday afternoon. He said that I should call his assistant and make an appointment, which I did the next morning.

Dean Epperson was the only black dean at the university at that time. He reminded me of our grade school principal in Japan who had, among other things, an advisory role for students. Dean Epperson's big smile and warm handshake immediately told me that he was happy to meet with me to answer my questions. I introduced myself as a senior at Carrollton State College of Pennsylvania majoring in psychology and told him I was exploring the possibility of enrolling into a master's degree program in social work.

"You said you wanted to know what makes social work so unique and special, right?" he asked. I nodded and opened my notebook I'd brought with me to take notes. He proceeded to tell me that social work practice is devoted to ethical principles at a much greater intensity and wider scope than other professions, as follows:

• Social work professionals serve people in need with integrity by showing individuals respect and honoring their dignity.

• Social workers are committed to the values of social justice and are required to be empathetic professionals; good listeners, who are able to understand a different person's point of view and understand their issues and problems from their perspective.

• Social work students are also trained to see the intrinsic value in every person and to do the right thing to help people help themselves. Students are taught how to work with humility and patience to inspire people and persuade individuals to change, resolve, or improve their conditions and circumstances.

• Genuine social workers do not pretend they are more knowledgeable than others, but rather are always available to actively listen and offer an individual hope.

• They are devoted to honesty, which is the most important factor in any human endeavor. Thus, social workers are eventually able to gain the trust of their community, and their clients in difficult situations. They are taught to be humble, compassionate, and dependable.

By the time students graduate with a master's degree in social work, they are also exposed to numerous social intervention theories and methods and know how to design studies to evaluate the outcome and impact of various interventions. Students often complained to faculty members that just during their first academic year, they were exposed to well over 10,000 pages of social work contents, which taught them how to use critical thinking strategies as they analyze social policies, afflicted communities, families, groups, and individuals, as well as society at large.

This conversation with Dean Epperson made me feel that pursuing a master's degree in social work was the right decision. However, he did warn me that the school had a high number of applicants in recent years, and he said that he had no influence over admission decisions.

I worked on my application for a whole week. I included an essay about why I wanted to attend Pitt's program, my transcripts, and my SAT results. I also obtained reference letters from my three favorite professors, from my economics, psychology, and calculus classes. My psychology professor sent me a copy of his reference letter, which noted that my performance in his class was in the top 1% of students he had taught during his nine years at the college. He also noted that because of my strength in the course, he requested that I help other students on the statistical analysis lessons. I was so grateful for his kind words and sent him a thank you letter for his generosity. I also thought that with such a good reference letter I would have no problem being admitted to the University of Pittsburgh School of Social Work.

But about four months later, I got my response from the admissions office. The program had rejected my application. The letter did not say why, except that they had a lot of applicants for the coming fall semester. Well, my immediate thought was about my grandfather's words about personal effort and *ganbate* "to never give up." I decided I wouldn't settle for their rejection—I immediately called and arranged for a meeting with the admissions director to discuss my application. His office was in the Cathedral of Learning, an imposing building near downtown Pittsburgh where many University of Pittsburgh classes were held.

Cathedral of Learning University of Pittsburgh

I was a bit nervous, but the admissions director was very gracious. He welcomed me into his office, which was decorated with pictures of his family and his son shooting a jump shot. I commented that my favorite sport is basketball and told him that I played as often as I could.

He smiled and said, "So, what can I do for you?" I told him that though I thought my grade point average and my reference letters must be okay, the school still rejected my application. He quickly pulled out my application that was already on his desk in a pile with several other folders. He reviewed my transcript and said, "I notice that you had attained As in your calculus, statistics, experimental psychology, and economics classes. Most social work applicants don't do well in those classes."

My English and literature classes during my freshman and sophomore years were not as good as I had hoped, however. I explained that my brother and I came to the US from Japan 10 years ago, and I was still learning how to write well because English is my second language.

He glanced at my reference letters and finally said, "I tell you what—our director of the research sequence major in social work may be interested in talking with you. His name is Dr. McBride, and his office is in Room 2210." He told me that if Dr. McBride accepted me into his courses, I would be admitted to the school. Then he told me to take my application folder to him to review.

"Tell him he can keep your application folder for now, but to let me know his decision as soon as possible," he said.

I was grateful and thanked him profusely for the opportunity. I leapt up the one flight of stairs to his department where I asked the receptionist for Dr. McBride. I told her that while I didn't have an appointment with him, it shouldn't take more than 10 minutes. She said that he was in class but that he should be done in about 20 minutes. Those 20 minutes seemed to last much longer. I was too nervous to anticipate what would happen in the meeting, but I spent the time finding the right words to convince him to accept my application.

Finally, Dr. McBride walked into the reception area. As he proceeded to check his mailbox the receptionist told him, "Dr. McBride, Mr. Yamada wants to meet with you for 10 minutes."

He glanced at me and said, "Ok, follow

me." He was a short black man with an afro and large glasses. He wore a relatively snug fitting shirt and dark blue jeans. Hanging all over his office walls were framed pictures of sports and civil rights leaders—Muhammad Ali alongside Joe Frazier, Malcolm X, and Rosa Parks. I was familiar with them since CSC had just celebrated Black History Month with various speakers who spoke about black leaders in the US. But I was a bit surprised that he didn't have a picture of Dr. Martin Luther King on his office desk or wall. However, I did know that Malcolm X and Dr. Martin Luther King did not see eye to eye, so he may have been partial to Malcolm X's more aggressive views.

He said in a deep voice, "What can I do for you?

I proceeded to explain that I was instructed by the admissions director to see him about potentially getting admitted to the MSW program. I told him that I was a psychology major in college but wanted to pursue a master's program in social work. He took my transcript and reviewed it with greater intensity than had the admission's director.

"Did you like statistics?" he asked.

"Yes, certainly more than my literature classes," I told him. "I am originally from Japan and am still learning English. So that explains some of my lower grades."

He also noted my score of nearly 700 on the SAT exam. "Wow," he said, "Among social work students, I haven't seen a score that high in several years. Do you think you would be interested in majoring in research in social work, and if so, why?"

I had to quickly figure out my best answer, and instantly, one of my grandfather's messages came to my mind.

"I believe knowledge and understanding is the key to solving a variety of social problems," I told him. "As my grandfather told me often: 'Knowledge is the greatest source of power.' Social research brings us closer to understanding more about society's problems, and I think such understanding will be the key towards solving them."

I also told Dr. McDaniel that one of my strengths is in data analysis and noted that I did well in experimental psychology—so well that, at the request of my professor, I tutored several students in the class.

After taking a few long agonizing moments to scan my application, he finally looked at me and said, "Congratulations. Your application is accepted."

He told me that I would be the 10th person enrolled in his program, which made up about 5 percent of the overall enrollment in the School of Social Work.

"I like to think that my students are elite neophytes," he said.

I immediately recognized the word "neophytes" from my exposure to the dreadful book we had to read in my high school: Ivanhoe by Water Scott. The book I hated ironically forced me to learn and appreciate a great word, "neophyte," which means someone who is new to a subject or mission. This experience reminded me that all knowledge is useful, but you never know when or for what reason.

With a smile, he told me that my tuition would be covered by the program's research grants and said that I would be one of his data analysis assistants. "I'll let the admissions director know that you've been admitted into my program," he said.

I happily thanked him. "My prayer has been answered by your kind decision," I told him. "Thank you again."

I immediately called Kathy from the

Cathedral of Learning's public phone booth and told her how my application status changed from rejection to acceptance with tuition coverage in less than three hours! She couldn't believe it.

"Your meeting with them really paid off!" she said.

I was amazed too. I told her we should celebrate that night, and I would pick her up to go to a steakhouse at 6 p.m.

Graduate school

My first class with Dr. McBride was memorable. My fellow students seemed a bit nervous about the course. I figured that might be because Dr. McBride would know how good we were as research majors and perhaps that might affect the full-tuition funding we would receive. The research grants provided enough funding to cover tuition and a monthly stipend of about $900 for all 10 students. I thought that no one in the class wanted to look incompetent or less intelligent than others, so we were indeed in competition with each other.

Introducing the class, Dr. McBride reviewed and summarized the major contents of the introductory research course that included basic statistical calculation methods. At one point, he asked the class if any of us knew what two to the ninth power is. At first, the class was silent; I realized nobody but me knew the answer. "Anyone?" Dr. McDaniel prompted. Finally, I was the only one to raise my hand and give the answer: "512."

Dr. McBride looked at me, surprised, and asked," How did you figure that out so quickly?"

I told him that we'd learned about exponential equations in seventh grade in Japan, and I remembered from all those years ago that two to the 10th power was 1024, so I knew to divide that by two to get to the ninth power: 512.

"You studied exponents in 7th grade?" he seemed dumbfounded.

I noticed some of my fellow students were glancing at each other with looks of amazement, but none of them looked happy about my mathematical skills. Seeing their faces, I started to feel a bit worried that my classmates would end up viewing me as one of those boring Asian nerds that no one would like. I didn't want to start school with such a false label, but it seemed unavoidable.

As I had feared, some of my research classmates seemed uncomfortable sitting with me at lunch, and few asked me to join them at after school events. As a minority, I could pick up on those negative vibes immediately. But I was also used to such treatment. I'd grown up feeling lonely due to being a parentless young child, so I didn't mind eating my lunch alone. I was completely at peace and felt comfortable without needing to enhance my social likeability to my fellow "neophytes."

My two-year master's program went smoothly, even though Dr. McBride made us take additional research related courses that were doctoral level in public health, educational research, sociology, and social psychology. As research majors, we did not have to take some of the standard courses most students were required to pass like clinical social work or community organization. By my final academic year, among 58 total required credits for graduation, about two-thirds of the courses were research related including social theories, measurement design, sampling methods, data processing software (e.g., SPSS and SAS), statistical data analysis, and a research internship.

Doctoral program?

Near the end of our final fall term, Dr. McBride guided me into his office and suggested that I should apply for our doctoral program. He said that he sat on the doctoral admissions committee, and the program had ample federal and local research grants to support my tuition and pay for a stipend. But he warned me that almost 40% of students fall short of earning their doctoral degree—typically because they fall short of completing their final dissertation. Those students were referred to as "all but dissertation (ABD)" candidates.

While doctoral students usually completed four to six years of school by the time they successfully defended their dissertation, Dr. McBride told me that he thought I'd be able to do the program within the scheduled four years.

"You're already better-trained than our typical doctoral applicants," he said. "Most other social work graduates don't have a master's degree in research."

I thanked Dr. McBride and left the room feeling lucky that he recognized my educational effort and commitment. Based on my quick calculations, if the doctoral program took four years, by the end, I would be in school a grand total of 24 years nonstop-beginning with grade school in Japan through my years of education in the US. I thought that my grandfather would be very proud. He had emphasized that "the scale of personal effort is an index of a person's greatness." I put in great effort to earn one of the highest possible educational degrees. My grandfather would have been proud of my commitment to hard work to achieve my goals.

I applied to the doctoral program, and for the first time in my higher education career, I was immediately accepted. The federal grants slated for all accepted doctoral students covered up to four years of tuition. As a doctoral research assistant, I was also given additional pay that was funded by one of the school's research projects that I worked on. It was an evaluation of a statewide private foster care program.

The project included a team of four doctoral students, including a project coordinator who was a third-year student, three research assistants, two second-year students, and myself. Our job was to outline the foster care program's major goals and translate them into measurable objectives to collect and analyze data to determine the program's effectiveness and success.

However, six months into the project, I recognized that our research coordinator was incompetent when it came to the application of research methods and data analysis. I felt that the project's almost two-month delay by the end of spring term was serious. This failure was primarily due to the coordinator's inability to organize, select appropriate measurement instruments, and choose strategies for comparative analyses.

I felt that this research ship could sink, mainly because the coordinator was unwilling to capitalize on the knowledge and suggestions of his capable research assistants and had selected a less than ideal research method. I voiced this concern with my fellow assistants several times, but they were unwilling to go directly to the director of our doctoral program and complain about the coordinator.

Because I was certain the project would fail, I decided to resign from working on it. I met and discussed my resignation with the director of our doctoral program and the research coordinator. The coordinator said he was very disappointed that I had decided to turn in my resignation, but he seemed comfortable with my request to no longer be on his research team. I was not so concerned about losing the stipend from this project because I figured I could do something else. My tuition was still covered by the federal grant.

This resignation meant that I could spend more time thinking about my final dissertation. The extra time I had in my schedule meant I might also be able to collect preliminary data to refine my research design and strategies. A fourth year doctoral student working on his own dissertation suggested that I should do all my coursework and assignments on the topic of my future dissertation study, so I would have reviewed the literature and theories and other pertinent information by the time I began my dissertation.

I also was informed that a local Catholic college for women about 30 miles away, southeast of Pittsburgh, called St. Drexel College for Women, was looking for someone to teach a course on social work research methods. Gaining teaching experience had always interested me because most doctoral graduates became teaching professors and researchers at universities. However, there were no courses offered for doctoral students to learn how to teach students in the program. Thus, I sent in my application to the Dean of Students at St. Drexel.

Within a week, the Dean of Students, Sister Turner, called and said she wanted to interview me for a position as an adjunct professor. St. Drexel College for Women had a total enrollment of just over 2,800 students. The college looked like a huge cathedral complex with several tall, sharply pointed roofs with gold crosses on top. Manicured trees surrounded the building complex and made the campus look peaceful and beautiful. The entrance to the building consisted of two huge doors. There was a half-dozen or so wide steps to the entrance doors where several students sat around to socialize.

As I entered the building, I was immediately greeted by a nun who said, "Welcome, how can I help you?"

I responded, "I'm here to meet with Sister Turner about teaching a course." As I was introduced to Sister Turner, I noticed how she looked astute in civilian attire—a woman's black business suit—and she spoke like a decisive administrator.

As I had hoped, the interview went very well, but I still remember one comment that stood out to me at the end of the interview.

"When you meet with a student in your office, please do not close the office door—keep it wide open," she told me. "Additionally, you as a professor should not accompany our students to lunch, dinner, or any other non-academic or recreational events." She looked at me as though she was saying, "Do you understand?"

I nodded and told her, "Sure no problem." I gathered that a Catholic women's college, more so than others, must be more sensitive to potential inappropriate relationships between professors and young female students.

So that fall, for the first time, I taught a class of 18 students—all young women—who made me self-conscious about how I may have looked to them as a Japanese man. The course was focused on my favorite subject: research methods, which made me somewhat more relaxed and enthused about teaching them. However, I did not realize how challenging it was to develop a lecture with various handouts and additional literature information. It took far more time than studying for doctoral level courses.

At my first session, I joked to my students, "I feel sorry for you. I'm originally from Japan, and so you must put up with my English being far from adequate," I warned them. "You should also know that more than likely I will not remember your names," I told them. "Just imagine, if I offered you 18 Japanese names, you might also have a difficult time remembering them!"

Some students chuckled in response.

"But that means you can be assured that your grade from me will be unbiased," I added, and more students laughed.

When I asked how many of the students thought they'd like the class, only two raised their hands. Finally, I asked the students which of them were afraid of the course and nearly every student raised their hand. I knew then that I had to make the class not only interesting but also well-organized and easy to understand.

At the end of the term, the students were required to evaluate the class. I was encouraged to find that, for the most part, they found my class to be informative and well-organized. They also rated my research knowledge high, and all said that they learned quite a lot. Some commented in writing that

I had a good sense of humor, and that my Japanese accent was not a problem.

Completing my dissertation

By the end of my third year in the doctoral program, I was ready to commence work on my dissertation. I had planned to do my dissertation studying the rampant overcrowding at Pennsylvania's state institutions for the severely mentally disabled, hoping to provide data to help officials make better decisions about how to best help them.

By then, I had preliminary data from a nearby state institution that served a similar population. The major problem for those institutions was that they were overcrowded, and their operational costs were growing out of control. The state policy makers wanted to reduce institutional overcrowding by limiting the residents of such institutions to only those who were severely mentally disabled and would not be able to live in community-based group homes. But Pennsylvania had no systematic way of determining which residents should be moved to group homes.

When I visited nearby institutions in Canonsburg and Franklin, the overcrowding was striking. Beds were pushed in together to squeeze in as many individuals into each room as possible. The two state-run institutions housed about 2,500 to 3,500 residents in total. My dissertation study needed to first develop an algorithm and matrix to identify an individual's level of functioning to determine who would be appropriate to move into a group home. I then compared the results by gender group to gauge the level of gender equity in the outcome. If my algorithm was unbiased, it would not favor male or female residents when selecting who would move to the group home and who would remain in the institution.

Because of my good research training, plus my data collection system with preliminary test findings, I was able to complete my dissertation within nine months. Thus, my doctoral education took four and a half years, as I had hoped.

Frustrating event

My only recollection of a bad experience during my doctoral studies occurred when my car (1965 Buick Skylark, which was 11 years old at that time) was stolen during the day. It was parked near our doctoral building on a street two blocks away. I walked around several blocks in disbelief. Initially I thought that I must have forgotten where I had parked. My mind refused to believe the possibility that it could have been stolen because such an occurrence had never happened to me. After 10 minutes or so of searching, I finally had to acknowledge that my car was gone. So I called Kathy and she suggested I should call Tom (my close high school friend) to pick me up since she was working until 9 p.m. that day.

That weekend I asked Tom if he would help me find the car since it could've been stolen to strip for parts—not for selling whole since the car was old. Starting that Saturday morning we drove around for several hours down just about every street within a five-to-six-mile radius. We finally found the car parked in an open lot with missing tires, battery, air cleaner, starter motor, FM radio, tape player, toolbox, and spare tire from its trunk, but otherwise, it was undamaged. So we drove to the Pitt police station and described where the car was and informed them that we would try to install the missing components on Sunday, and get the car started.

We then went immediately to purchase the critical parts from the local auto parts store and repair shop, and, by Tom's suggestion, a five-gallon gas can because he warned that thieves may have siphoned out the gas. On that Sunday we arrived early to reinstall the missing parts. As we were installing the parts, I noticed that several cars with teenagers and young adults passed by and some seemed to be smiling as they proceeded. Luckily, after filling it with the five-gallon gas can the car did start but this would happen again.

A week later, my car was stolen. Apparently, the same thieves knew that I had mounted new rims with tires, a new battery, starter motor, and other items. So, this time I knew where to go first to find the car, and I was right. Tom and I, again, replaced the necessary items and re-reported the theft to the police, who said that if the new tires and rims surfaced, they would immediately let me know. However, as expected, the police never called me with good news. But now I decided to be smarter. Even though I had to pay a monthly fee, I parked in a covered parking lot from that day on. You live and you learn.

Chapter 12

ENGAGEMENT TO KATHY AND OUR WEDDING

D URING MY DOCTORAL program years, Kathy and I continued to date and coped with the fact that she attended a university 75 miles away. During sunny weekends, I would drive my Honda motorcycle to her campus and take her out for dates, often to Cheat Lake for swimming, or Coopers Rock Park for picnicking (both were located five to six miles from her campus).

Kathy at the Cheat Lake

As I was seeing her on a continuous basis, I noticed that just about every activity felt like a new adventure, even ordinary things like going together to a grocery store, doing laundry, visiting friends, attending church, etc. I felt an inner happiness as she held my hand and said my name, simple things, but they felt so good. Her presence made me feel that I needed to be a better person: good, kind, and thoughtful. Even when things went wrong, like my car refusing to start in the rain, I noticed that we did not mind missing our dinner reservation as we waited for the slow arriving AAA service. I also started to generate my own thoughts about our future, such as building a new house, taking vacation trips to Japan and other exotic countries, and raising children. As I mentioned such dreams of mine to her, it was thrilling to hear her say, "That sounds great." I was ready to be her husband and wanted us to get engaged.

After going to five or six jewelry stores, I found a ring that was artistically arranged and beautiful. I also wrote down exactly what I would say to ask Kathy to marry me. I planned out just how I would do it and practiced my speech a dozen times. Amazingly, I still remember those words like an old favorite song that never leaves you.

One late September day, I drove my car to her campus and took her to one of the most expensive restaurants in town. After dinner, we took a walk in a well-lit park. The moon was shining bright, and sparkling stars filled the night sky. The slightly chilly, fresh air made the evening feel even more romantic. After a brief walk, at the right moment, I took her hand and got down on my knees. She seemed surprised; she looked at me and simply said, 'What are you doing?"

"Kathy, I would like today to be the beginning of us together so I can revolve around you eternally. I want to make my heart to be your home and see you there endlessly. I love you more than anything in the world, and I will work relentlessly to be the right person for your life. Kathy, will you marry me?"

Tears streamed down her cheeks, creating shining paths on her beautiful face.

"Yes!" she cried. "I love you very much, Hide."

Hearing her say these words, my heart filled with elation. I felt myself elevated to a higher dimension. All I wanted from that moment on was to make her happy forever and to live a life of enlightenment together.

We kissed and hugged, and I held her hand and placed the ring on her finger. It looked even more beautiful on her hand.

"It's beautiful," she sighed. "I love it."

I told her that I had a mini bottle of cold champagne in the car, to celebrate. As we sat on a bench and shared the glass of Champagne, I felt infinitely blessed to be with this wonderful and special person. When she hugged me, she made me feel, beyond a doubt, that I was a far more desirable and better man.

The next morning, I called my mother, brother, and my friends and said, "I have never been this happy in my entire life; Kathy and I got engaged last night." Kathy also called her mom, sister, and her best friend Mary as well. They were all congratulatory, especially my brother and my friends. And they wanted to know the wedding date.

Kathy noted that she would be graduating early, by December 1973 because she had taken extra courses throughout college. She also noted that right after her graduation her parents wanted her to come to Washington, D.C., where they had recently moved from Pittsburgh, and look for a job with one of the federal agencies.

But she had already rejected their suggestion. She instead wanted to find a job in Pittsburgh and planned to live with her best friend Mary from high school. Kathy intended to look for a teaching job or some other position in the public school system.

We ultimately decided that our wedding would be in April of 1974 because we thought that would give Kathy some time to start her career after graduating. If all went well, we would be a young 21- and 26-year-old married couple.

In December, as planned, Kathy began looking for a public-school job in the Pittsburgh area. It was a challenging time to enter the workforce because the US was in the midst of a recession. In fact, 1974 was a year of rising prices and rising unemployment, at the same time. Nearly 300,000 school employees in the US had lost their jobs. Schools were also financially dependent on state governments, and they were particularly vulnerable to the recession.

Despite such a difficult economic situation, Kathy was able to secure substitute-teaching positions in several high schools. It was a job, but her salary was much lower than what full-time teachers earned, so she kept looking for other employment possibilities. Several weeks before our wedding date, she was hired by the huge Kaufman's Department Store that occupied an entire block in downtown Pittsburgh, to work as a restaurant manager and an assistant to the director of the store's food service. It was a substantial operation, with 11 restaurants, one large bakery and several cookie, pie, popcorn, and hotdog stations. She oversaw 400 staff members including chefs, bakers, waiters and waitresses, and other support workers.

As the wedding day approached, the only concern I had about us was how Kathy would handle the challenges of being part of a mixed-race couple. Walking together down the street, our differences were very noticeable. She had porcelain skin with bright red hair, while my hair was black, and I obviously looked Japanese (or Asian). She looked like a beautiful Irish girl, even though she also had some German and Czechoslovakian in her ancestry.

I remember how frightened we were one time while visiting Uniontown, PA. We rode into the town on my motorcycle, Kathy riding in back, and the traffic slowed to a near stop. Up ahead, we could see a large cross 10 to 15 feet high hoisted into the ground with a half-dozen or so KKK members in their all-white attire, wearing pointed caps and collecting contributions from everyone driving through town. Such an event was relatively uncommon, but some towns in the southwest region of Pennsylvania and nearby West Virginia had so many KKK members (often including their mayor, police chief, and town's council members) that they considered the KKK as a group with a right to collect money from the public for their organization. I knew that if they saw Kathy and me together, they might assault us.

"Try looking away from the guys," I whispered to Kathy. "Our helmets may help us hide our faces." I pulled out a dollar bill, quickly stuffed it into their bucket, and drove off. I think one KKK member did notice us, but he said nothing.

Kathy in downtown Pittsburgh

On many occasions we had to watch how waiters and waitresses reacted when we entered a restaurant. If they seemed uneasy that a mixed-race couple was about to order a meal, we looked for another one. Such episodes were especially frequent in West Virginia during the early 1970s.

Several months before the wedding day, we met with a Catholic priest in Eastwood, Pennsylvania, as required by the Catholic church, to let him know of our intent to marry. Disappointingly, the priest—who must have been 70 years old or so—tried to discourage us by asking seemingly poorly-chosen questions.

"Have you thought about how your children would feel being mixed race?" he asked. "How would their peers treat the children since they will be different from their peers? Did you know mixed marriages have a much higher divorce rate than other same-race couples?"

He was careful not to tell us outright that we shouldn't get married, but his implications were obvious. Thank goodness we only had decided to meet with him for convenience since Kathy had planned to visit me that weekend, and my apartment was located only five blocks from the church.

In any case, Kathy always wanted to get married in her hometown, Johnstown, PA. Kathy's family had attended church there prior to moving to Pittsburgh. Kathy's grandmother still lived there and had an amicable relationship with the head Catholic priest at the church.

Since we were genuinely in love, I was confident about my ability to effectively deal with any potential challenges or disputes resulting from others' bigotry. And because I was informed about racism and bigotry from my grandfather and my own experiences, I was prepared for resistance and disapproval from others. I practiced remaining centered: avoiding anger and maintaining a rational mind in the face of any such situation. That meant that I didn't lose sleep over facing any loathsome behavior.

But for Kathy, who hadn't grown up coping with bigotry, I thought only time would tell how she would handle undignified treatment from people suffering with narrow-minded prejudice. Like my grandfather often said:

Time unveils everything. The truth has a way of surfacing clearly in time. This applies to the commitments of people, quality of relationships, and words of experts and leaders, as well.

He also cautioned me: "So be careful. if you are not being sincere and truthful, it will reveal itself for others to clearly see and realize in time."

Memorable wedding

Our wedding day, April 27, 1976 was unusually beautiful—a blue-sky, sunny and warm. We couldn't believe that we'd be blessed with such a perfect day for our wedding.

St. John Gualbert Co-Cathedral in Johnstown, where we had our wedding, was built in the shape of a cross with the top of the cross facing west. The church was a gothic style facility with stone walls and wide and dark front steps. The east end of the church held the altar where the bread and wine are sanctified. As the wedding guests arrived and were ushered to the right seating side, I had requested to play through the church's sound system my special music selection: Preludium in E Major by Eugene Ormandy & The Philadelphia Orchestra. This is one of the music selections that was in my father's album that got "lost" during our trip to the US. It is an upbeat orchestral arrangement that I thought was perfectly suited for guests filing into their seats. Then Kathy's selection—Allegro Maestoso by George F. Handel—followed. That piece sounded much more formal, but it was still joyful, and perfect for the wedding party to walk down the center aisle and line up just below the church's altar.

As the organist started to play "The Wedding March" by Mendelssohn, guests stood and turned towards the church's entryway

to honor Kathy as she was being escorted
by her father. Standing at the altar, I carefully
watched her walk up the aisle. I felt overjoyed
as I fought to control my tears at the beautiful
sight of her in her wedding dress. The wedding
gown was long and lacy with a classic long veil
that Kathy had made entirely by herself. I was
astonished when she told me that she planned
to design and make her wedding gown instead
of wearing a ready-made dress from a bridal
shop. This task required almost six months to
finish, but it was completed just the way she
wanted. It was stunning.

Kathy's wedding dress

As Kathy and her dad marched closer to the altar, I noticed that she looked confident and proud. She seemed to know that her wedding dress was perfect, and that she looked fit to appear as a beautiful bride. In contrast, her father appeared joyless as he cautiously escorted Kathy. As he guided her hand to me, I noticed that his left hand was shaking slightly, and (I may be mistaken but) he looked unsure.

As the priest announced us as husband and wife and we kissed, I felt very gratified but also contemplative. As we turned around and faced almost 100 nearly all white attendants in the church, my immediate thought was that I now have the awesome future responsibility of making sure that Kathy remains safe, happy, and satisfied with her life as part of a mixed-race couple.

Mas was my best man, and Kathy's maid of honor was her older sister, Chris. We invited my best friends, mainly from my college and my fraternity, about 30 or so altogether, and they dominated my side of the church since only four other guests were directly from my family. My brother and his wife Bunny, along with my mother and stepfather. The bride's group was more than twice as large as my side—about 70 or so attendees.

We held the wedding reception at a beautiful countryside restaurant called Green Gables. The large reception room had shining marble stone floors with massive load-bearing pillars spaced around the room. Large windows looked out over a picturesque pond with a pathway near the center. The room was full of round tables featuring gold dinner plates, specially ordered wrought iron bistro chairs, and beautiful floral centerpieces at each table. We hosted a sit-down dinner where the guests were served a stuffed pork chop accompanied by fresh green beans by about a dozen waiters and waitresses in formal-looking black uniforms.

I was impressed and thankful that Kathy's parents went all out and arranged for what looked like a very expensive wedding reception (later Kathy mentioned that it was expensive). While Kathy had a lot to do with the planning and decor, her parents still agreed to pay the huge bill from Green Gables.

The wedding reception went as well as we could hope for. There was a lot of joyful conversation and laughter, and many congratulatory handshakes and hugs. After our first dance, Mas and Bunny and my friends seemed to be having a great time dancing. Near the end of the reception, the DJ stopped playing, and my fraternity brothers all came together on the dance floor and sang to Kathy a special "Sweetheart Song," which is our fraternity's traditional song about how fortunate we all are to have a beautiful person like you as the sweetheart of our dear brother. I think she had to fight back tears as their words seemed to touch her heart. They sounded fabulous—sincere and genuine.

Many of Kathy's guests came to the bride and groom's table to congratulate us and offer their best wishes. Some asked where we were going for our honeymoon, and Kathy told them that we had plans to travel after I finished my dissertation, but we had no idea where to go yet.

Our wedding photo at Green Gables

Meanwhile, soon after the dinner and cake-cutting ceremony, I noticed that both my mother and stepfather were beginning to look uncomfortable. They were very quiet and reserved—they'd made no effort to talk to Kathy's family members. They only responded with smiles to the guests visiting their table. I doubt if my mother even exchanged words of thanks to Kathy's mother and father. My stepfather looked as though he couldn't wait to get home.

However, I wondered what was in my mother's thoughts as she watched her oldest son (and previously Mas) marry for love, far less encumbered by family dictates and diminished options than she faced as a Japanese Catholic single mother. Even knowing about the potentially difficult road ahead for both of us, as well as our future mixed-race children, I surmised she may have been relieved that we would not be lonely—a difficulty that she had to negotiate for much of her life.

As the reception got closer to its end, my brother Mas and Bunny came toward us. Grasping my shoulder, he said, "I wish you all the happiness, just like I have with my wife, Bunny." Kathy and I hugged them and walked over to Kathy's parents and thanked them as well. Waving our hands to the guests, we departed the memorable reception.

Chapter 13

MY CAREER

I COMPLETED MY doctoral program in 1976. At the time, the nation was again going through an economic stagnation and recession, and a majority of universities across the country were not yet ready to begin hiring new and additional faculty members. I looked for just about any job to pass the time until an assistant professor position became available. After about a month of searching for employment, I accepted a position as a research consultant at the University of Pennsylvania working on a federally funded grant project. We were tasked with conducting a statewide assessment of the knowledge and skill levels of human service workers who were employed by the Pennsylvania Department of Public Welfare (PADPW) and employees of major organizations contracted by PADPW.

This job required an assessment of well over 50,000 social service providers' training needs, and an estimation of the training budget for each of the 67 counties in Pennsylvania. Pennsylvania had received a $20 million Title 20 grant from the US Congress to implement this statewide training program. To make a long story short, my job was to help develop the statewide training needs assessment instrument, help coordinate the data collection, write a statistical algorithm for gauging the magnitude of training needs, and estimate training budgets for each county in Pennsylvania. This job was a perfect fit with what I had specialized in during my doctoral program.

I enjoyed working with the statewide training department in Harrisburg for nearly two years. I developed a strong relationship with the director and the training department, as well as his top-level staff members. They frequently invited me to their homes, and together we enjoyed local events (e.g., the annual statewide farm show, circus events, classic car shows, etc.). I still have fond memories from the experience and appreciate many of those kind people. The director of the department still sends me friendly emails from time to time, even after over 40 years since I left the job. The only hardship was that I had to get an apartment in Harrisburg and have dinners by myself most of the week, and sleep alone until I came home on weekends to Pittsburgh.

Obviously, Kathy and I did not like being apart during the week, but we simply had to make the best of it. Calling her every evening and conversing about each other's day reassured and comforted me. It strengthened our relationship in a way, and our spiritual connection with each other. As my grandfather taught me, through spiritual self-reflection of your life, you will become a strong and resilient individual and maintain a much-needed internal balance.

A message from Dean Epperson

After almost two years of working in Harrisburg, I got a call from Dean Epperson, who had initially guided me to consider the social work profession. He indicated that the School of Social Work at the University of Pittsburgh would be hiring one assistant level professor starting that fall term and that I should consider applying. I immediately called him the next morning and said, "First of all, thank you very much for kindly extending this critical message. I will definitely apply for the position."

However, like in our first meeting, he said, "You should know that I have no control in selecting the three finalists by the school's recruitment committee. But I get to select one of three finalists to be hired for our Provost's approval."

I thanked him profusely and immediately called Kathy and told her that we were blessed: "There is an assistant professor position open at the University of Pittsburgh School of Social Work, and I think I have a remote chance to be hired."

Kathy responded, "Great, but why do you think you have only a remote chance?" I explained that the University of Pittsburgh, like other great universities across the country, has a policy of not hiring their own doctoral graduates in order to avoid a saturation of homogeneous perspectives among the faculty members. If the selected finalist happens to be their own doctoral graduate, the dean's office must produce a document justifying reasons why, and the provost's committee must review the request for their own assessment, which is then forwarded to the provost for the ultimate decision.

I had heard of this policy during my time as a doctoral student, so I told Kathy that we could only remain cautiously hopeful. My estimated probability of being selected through the hiring review process was only 12.5%, and the probability of the recruitment committee selecting my application as one of three finalists through the provost's approval was still low, 25%. Except for one full professor, there were no doctoral graduates hired at the time working as an assistant or associate professor at the school.

To my deep appreciation, I was selected as a new assistant professor with the provost's approval among several dozen applicants reviewed by the recruitment committee. Apparently, the school needed a faculty member who specialized in data management, writing statistical algorithms, and who would be comfortable using both parametric (based on bell-shaped data distribution) and non-parametric statistical procedures (based on probability). Their faculty members specializing in research methods were generally unfamiliar with arrays of nonparametric statistical procedures that are often more relevant in community-based social work research.

Even with an amazing outcome that brought such great joy for Kathy and I, I was saddened at the same time that my grandfather, who had so much to do with my efforts through twenty-four years of school, was no longer with us to share this joy. I was denied the chance to thank him, to share this accomplishment with him. He effectively taught me to focus on personal effort ("index of greatness") and on becoming a centered person (e.g., importance of integrity, earning people's trust, and remember that, "None of us are ever finished with self-improvements," and "An inferior human trait to be avoided is arrogance.").

From the beginning of my career at the University of Pittsburgh I was determined to prove that the recruitment committee and Dean Epperson did not make a mistake in selecting me as a new assistant professor. In part, this personal commitment was confirmed by the associate dean and faculty executive committee's findings that I was teaching more students in research courses (per class enrollment subscription) than any of my colleagues, and my student evaluation ratings for these research courses were the highest among my counterparts teaching same courses.

When the Director of Data Management left the job for a better paying position offered to him by the Carnegie Museum, I was asked by the dean to temporarily oversee the system until they hired a replacement. I took this opportunity to help with the school's data management system. Unfortunately, the University consistently had to reduce annual budgets across schools and departments for the subsequent ten years, an era of "doing more with less." So, for ten years I was the school's only data management specialist; a job added to my regular duties. I also served on countless time-consuming doctoral dissertation committees and guided various research projects to their completion. All my advisees passed their final dissertation defense when so many others failed to complete theirs. I also kept conducting my own research and continued publishing peer-reviewed journal articles.

Soon after receiving my tenured associate professor status, I decided that I should further expand my specialization in my career field— evaluation of social services and optimization of organizational performance. Additionally, what was rare among non-profit organizations was the lack of performance strategies practiced by for-profit organizations. Most non-profit organizations at that time rarely scientifically evaluated the impact of their services to their clients and virtually never assessed organizations' adequacies of quality assurance systems, supervisory competence, and work culture and climate. They also often neglected assessments of factors associated with service constraints or needs for collaborations with other service providers. Thus, I applied to the graduate school of business' Executive MBA program, which was designed as a weekend-only program to benefit employed candidates.

My application was partially rejected. The letter from the admissions committee indicated that its executive MBA class was already full, but the committee had approved my application for enrolling into the regular full-time or part-time MBA program. So, I accepted the three-year, part-time MBA program.

It was nice to be taught instead of teaching students. I enjoyed most of the MBA classes except the accounting courses, which were not based on scientific knowledge but annually adjusted tax law procedures. There is not much scientific exploration in applying accounting procedures. You simply have to remember and incorporate all the new regulations that are fueled by political forces.

Learning about strategies for attaining business success gave me what my grandfather had always preached to me: knowledge is the greatest source of power. However, one must go beyond knowing to understand the knowledge. That is a higher human insight, which allows for real value enhancement— to successfully apply the knowledge in order to achieve targeted goals. With my MBA experience, I felt that I was closer to understanding how to start helping solve the challenges faced by social and human service organizations. Many of them were struggling to effectively serve communities suffering from relentless poverty and its associated afflictions. Their client outcomes, post discharge, were often less than optimal to warrant continual funding support.

University of Hawaii?

Soon after earning an MBA degree,

someone must have referred my name, and I received a request that I consider sending my CV to the recruitment committee of the University of Hawaii. Since Hawaii is one of the most beautiful places to live and less than halfway between Pittsburgh and Japan, I wanted to know what the university thought of my qualifications. The chair of their recruitment committee contacted me to schedule an interview at the next national conference meeting in Washington, D.C. I agreed. I thought I had nothing to lose by hearing what they had to say. A week after my interview, they offered me an associate professor's position pending my reference letters with the request to immediately call their dean for more details.

The dean at the University of Hawaii indicated that if I chose their university, my salary would be higher than most other universities because of the higher cost of living in Hawaii. She quoted a salary offer that was $10,000 higher than what I was earning at Pitt. So right after the interview, per proper protocol, I notified my dean that the University of Hawaii offered me an associate professor's position.

The next day, Dean Epperson called me

into his office. At that meeting, the memorable and much-appreciated comment he made to me was, "I have learned over the years that if you want to get things done right, give the project to the busiest person, and that one of hard-working faculty members at our school is you." He also informed me that he had already touched base with the provost's office to increase my salary to the same amount as Hawaii's offer. I had no second thoughts; I gratefully accepted his offer.

I was promoted to full professor in 1993 by Pitt's tenure and promotion committee together with my closest colleagues, Drs. Gary Koeske and Lambert Maguire. This was especially joyful because their friendship was an invaluable part of my experience while working at the University. We frequently went to lunch and talked about everything from our families to discussions about our research and the University. Together we also attended most of the University's sponsored events (e.g., the annual picnic, lecture series, and research-related workshops) and most national conferences.

I was also fortunate to be selected for major evaluative research grants (e.g., assessments of United Way's services for substance addicted young mothers with children, quality of life among federal housing communities, estimation of effective caseload among the county's children, youth, and family workers, reviewing the Allegheny County Jail Collaborative with the mission of reducing former inmates' recidivism rates, measuring the effectiveness of huge foster care organizations, etc.). In large part, however, my success as professor and researcher was due to the instrumental assistance by the University's deans, key staff members, and my careful selection and hiring of the right staff assistants who effectively managed my research tasks, edited my reports and journal articles, and assisted in writing grant proposals. I am compelled to name these key people (in alphabetical order): Hailey Jung, Barbara Keaton, Judy Latta, Regina Lyons, Jan Mac Gregor, Marcia Piel, Sue Scheuring, Solveig Spjeldnes, Megan Soltesz, Jennifer Thornton, Melissa Wilk, and Michele Zorich. I owe much of my achievements to these super intelligent, creative, and dedicated individuals.

Every so often as I walked out of my car from the Soldiers and Sailors underground parking facility, I would look up at the

Cathedral of Learning building and say to myself, "I have the best job in the world—I feel so lucky and happy to be here."

Consultation job

Perhaps due to my teaching specialization, I kept receiving consulting requests to evaluate local social and human service programs. The demand for my help became so substantial that, for tax purposes, I decided to start an S-corporation called Excellence Research, Inc. (ERI). My focus was conducting evaluation projects for non-profits. I believe such a demand evolved because so many of my former students had secured staff positions with social and human service organizations across the region. I also had a substantial number of subsequent repeat requests. These episodes made me feel that I had to work even harder and with more passion at the University so that no one would doubt my commitment to the School of Social Work. Although website-based business advertisements had become very popular during my ERI start-up, I decided not to use this strategy. Instead, I just relied on my "word of mouth" reputation from previous consulting customer organizations. This decision was based on a concern that some of the provost's office administrators might incorrectly interpret my career commitment as self-serving (ERI) and that my university job was a secondary employer. Additionally, at the end of every academic year, I reported all my completed consulting projects to the dean's office to stay as transparent as possible.

Overall, these evaluation opportunities with various organizations (e.g., Carnegie Science Center, Center Against Domestic and Sexual Abuse, Community Empowerment Association, Make-A-Wish Foundation, Negro Emergency Education Drive, Pennsylvania Organization for Women in Early Recovery, Salvation Army, Southwestern PA AIDS Coalition, Tadiso - formerly Pittsburgh Black Action, Inc., YWCA of Pittsburgh, and 30 or so others) further increased my knowledge and understanding about how to help optimize organizational performance through an evaluation process. Additionally, this experience immensely helped my teaching and scholarly writing. As my grandfather had noted an important distinction, I was able to ascend from just having knowledge of evaluation to understanding how to generate helpful, evidence-based evaluation reports that were focused on how to further improve and effectively achieve their organizational goals.

Taking on key roles

As a full professor, I kept super busy and played a major role in the department's operations. For example, I served as the chairperson of the Accreditation Review Committee. This involved submitting extensive documentation of our undergraduate and master's programs to continue our accreditation. The application for accreditation included approximately 2,500 single spaced reports, and for the first time in the previous 24 years (1988 to 2012), the School of Social Work was approved for accreditation with no required revisions.

As the school's Associate Dean for Research, my responsibility was to guide and assist faculty members' scholarly projects. My major accomplishments in this role were not only significantly increasing the number of funded research projects, but I was able to persuade faculty members to collaborate and include other faculty members on their research studies. This expanded the percentage of faculty members involved in scholarly research from around 28% to over 40%. The provost also required each school to generate their own strategies and evaluate their outcomes for further advancements in faculty scholarship, student learning, and securing research grants. As the chair of the Strategic Planning Committee, within eight years we were able to double the amount of faculty members' rate of scientific publications, which resulted in the 6th highest publication rate among schools in the nation compared to our 42nd rating just before I took on this role.

We also continually increased student satisfaction ratings, helpfulness of their academic advisers, adequacy of academic culture of the school, and support of all students by gender, racial/ethnic, and sexual orientation. We ascended our national ranking of overall school quality from 14th (when I started) to the much more appealing 10th among over 210 social work graduate schools in the nation. We were also ranked first in the state of Pennsylvania amongst well-known public institutions and private institutions (e.g., University of Pennsylvania, known as Penn, Bryn Mawr University, Temple University, etc.). It should be noted that without the leadership of our Dean Larry Davis, the successor to Dean Epperson, and the dedication of faculty members, such accomplishments would have been unrealized.

I also chaired other committees that virtually no one wanted to lead including Tenure and Promotion, Quality Assurance, Budget Review and Planning, Scientific Review, and Data Management. Every Wednesday, all these committees met for discussions and task planning. I practiced going to my meetings with solutions to the problem or challenges and ending meetings by summarizing a list of what needed to be done, by whom, and by when to save time rather than pondering what we should do. I rarely needed to meet for more than 30 minutes or so in each of the committees that I chaired. A memorable comment made by a faculty member about my committee meetings was, "If you are late for Dr. Yamada's meeting by 10 minutes, you missed the meeting."

I can honestly declare that I enjoyed highly satisfying work life at the University of Pittsburgh. I believe that my satisfaction resulted from choosing to focus my efforts on serving the School of Social Work the best I could. As my grandfather had noted, "Life satisfaction emanates from serving others, not through self-serving." I noticed this insight at play among our faculty members— even though being a faculty member of a well-ranked University is one of the best jobs in the world, those who seemed to give the least effort were generally more dissatisfied with their job.

Chapter 14

MUCH AWAITED TRAVEL BACK TO JAPAN

A s our careers progressed enough to start increasing our savings, an important goal was to travel more domestically and eventually to Japan. So we kept saving to visit various places including San Francisco, Los Angeles, Lake Tahoe, Yosemite National Park, Las Vegas, Fort Worth and Dallas Texas, NY City, Atlantic City, Lake Placid NY, Philadelphia, Washington DC, etc. We were also finally able to visit Japan and Hawaii in July 1980.

My extended family in Japan (1980)

When visiting Japan, we were careful not to stay with our relatives long because if we did, they would control our schedule. We limited our family time to a mere long weekend (Friday to Monday) including visiting my grandparents' Catholic burial site.

At the cemetery

When we arrived at the cemetery, I was surprised by how beautifully the pine trees and flowering shrubberies were artistically arranged and manicured.

As we located my grandparents' marble tombstone, I could not hold back my tears. I was suddenly hit by a sense of overwhelming joy as well as remorse for not taking care of my grandfather. As a young boy I was too focused on reuniting with my mother to appreciate what I already had. I stood there and cried as Kathy held me, also feeling her own joy and sadness for me. Many memories of my life with him sprung up—his smile, adoring facial expressions, engaging eyes, soft voice, his big hand holding mine, and his angry face when I misbehaved. Those memories had never gone away. I kneeled and prayed that he would see us here from his good place in Heaven and hear my words of love and appreciation. I told him that I did not realize how good of a man he really was until I got older and began to understand his Words of Understanding.

Soon, the rain started and we had to walk back to our car. Seiko had arranged a big dinner for us to further commemorate my extended family members (aunts, including Catholic nuns and cousins). Most of our conversation centered around what it was like to live in the US and how our neighbors and friends treated my wife Kathy. All we could say to them was that we felt very fortunate that we are able to sustain our happiness as a married couple. It was nice that there was no disapproval from my extended Japanese family members because Kathy is an American. In fact, the opposite was true: they adored her. Such reactions reminded me of my grandfather's notation that, "War is between governments, not between people of the countries like us."

On Monday morning we said our goodbyes to our relatives and began to travel to a few select destinations including Fukuoka, Yamamoto, Kyoto, Nara, and Tokyo on Japan's well-known bullet trains, which traveled well over 200 miles per hour. The train was impressively clean, comfortable and had a waitress for small meals and beverages. In addition to Japanese, the train's alerts were in English and French, which was a noticeable advancement from 1961 when we left for the U.S.

Our bullet train

When we got off at the Kyoto train station, I unknowingly handed in my Tokyo tickets instead of my Kyoto tickets. After a one-day visit, we got on the bullet train to return to Tokyo. When the conductor asked us to show our tickets, I was shocked to find that we did not have the right tickets. I explained what I thought had happened. The conductor immediately called the Kyoto station and within 15 minutes or so, they were able to locate our tickets and send in our right numeric codes for our Tokyo trip. I was impressed that they were so efficiently accommodating. I thought that Japan was clearly incorporating new technology and making advancements.

Visiting various destinations in Japan with Kathy was, to say the least, wonderful. We found that so many Japanese people were quite friendly to American visitors. For example, when we got lost in Tokyo, a young man not only told us how to get to the train station, but he took his time and led us seven blocks to the right station so we would not get lost. Japanese streets are the opposite of, say, the city streets of Chicago. No street goes straight for long, and it is a maze with lots of alleyways where you can easily get lost. A passing young man was so interested in practicing his English that he asked Kathy if we could share a coffee at his expense. I was disappointed that he only looked at Kathy as he issued this offer. Later I told Kathy, "Maybe I should wear a sign that says I am a Japanese-American so I can get an offer for free coffee."

As we departed Japan, I felt very happy

that we visited my grandparents' burial site and spent time in a spiritual retreat. I needed this event to finally free my soul of the regrets that I had long harbored since his passing. My chest felt lighter and divinely revived. I felt healthier realizing that, even without his physical presence, finally, our souls met. As I visualized him looking down from his place in Heaven, I intuited his adoring contentment, which was a crucially missing component in my pursuit of harmony. I wanted to make my grandfather proud.

Introspection

As I got older and started to understand more about my grandfather's teachings, I came to realize that harmony begins with the ability to remain centered: a sense of composure and peace with oneself. Personal challenges and problems are to be handled with flexibility, tolerance, and good thoughts. Personal harmony requires gentleness in judgment and lenience in one's assessment of self and others, to continually enrich self-understanding and nurture important relationships. One must also be able to let go of past problems and be open to new changes with the hope of a brighter future. Most people find that it is difficult to maintain a good relationship with those who suffer from continuous and hopeless pessimism.

To attain personal comfort and security, harmonious people must also associate with other harmonious people and cultivate these rewarding relationships. Sharing time with friends to appreciate simple natural pleasures such as beautiful lakes, fantastic mountains, the stunning moon, millions of dazzling stars, alluring sunrises, and sunsets can further enhance a sense of wellness and delight. Harmonious individuals tend to be generous people who selflessly perform good deeds. They invite connection with people of various backgrounds and life situations and avoid submitting to toxic arrogance.

However, I also understand that none of us is immune from personal problems, failures, and other disruptive issues that can make it difficult to remain centered. At some point in life, each of us will face challenges, such as family crises, economic challenges, social/institutional setbacks, health-related predicaments, or spirit-crushing life complexities (e.g., enduring hate, persistent disgust, loss of faith, etc.). To survive these challenges, one must understand what constitutes happiness, life satisfaction, and the need for renewed centering.

During my childhood in Japan, the encouragement I received from my grandparents, Mas, and aunt Seiko, protected me from emotional collapse. Even though I struggled to cope with my parents' absence, my family's nurturing and guidance helped me to grow up safe and mature into my teen years.

I also believe that my grandfather's teachings helped advance my emotional and interpersonal IQ. From him I learned how to be cognizant of others' feelings and needs and to treat people with sensitivity and respect. Stemming from this knowledge grew my understanding about how to manage my daily challenges.

There is one task that all of us continually face, no matter what we do for a living (e.g., teachers, bankers, researchers, book writers, lawyers, social workers, public administrators, nurses, parents, consultants, and others). If you cannot meet this challenge properly, your insights, competence, knowledge, creativity, and skills may have a significantly diminished impact, possibly no impact at all. What is this challenge?

It is to persuade others.

How valuable is a teacher who cannot persuade students to learn? How successful are parents if they cannot persuade their kids to focus on being a good person? How effective is a counselor who cannot persuade clients to follow through with their intervention protocols? And how effective are lawyers if they cannot persuade the jury to believe their points of view?

As a mixed-race couple, I was fortunate that Kathy and I agreed that the worst human trait is arrogance that produces false feelings of superiority over others. Her love never ceased and her happiness in our marriage has persuaded me to view myself as a desirable and worthy person. She has consistently worked to be the right person for my life and me. Her knowledge and understanding about child development also boosted our children's self-confidence and inspired them to persistently pursue and reach their goals. She also effectively persuaded them to value themselves and to become good individuals.

So, what are the key elements for successfully persuading others? Just about all the insights outlined in the Words of Understanding. Those include earning the trust of others through dignified thoughts and behavior, acquiring knowledge and understanding, working hard, and practicing honesty, respect, and compassion towards others. Without earning or gaining the trust of others you will not effectively persuade them. Thus, harmony cannot be attained unless you are able to persuade others of your genuinely good intent. Having others appreciate your stature, uniqueness, and vision helps you to progress towards achieving personal harmony. Continual rejection and neglect by others can invite undesirable feelings of imbalance and dissonance.

Was my grandfather mistaken?

As repeatedly noted, I was so fortunate to have my grandfather's love and guidance during my early childhood days. His Words of Understanding helped me to practice centering and enabled me to face my challenges from the day of our arrival in the US through to the post-retirement phase of my life. However, he miscalculated one major factor.

Due to the historical accounts of the US-Japan relationships and how US citizens and their public leaders treated Japanese Americans at the time, he was deeply concerned about the cultural and social difficulties we could face in the US. He was worried that we had no understanding of the potentially devastating impact of racial bigotry and the enormous coping efforts that would be needed to manage prejudice and intolerance. For this reason he suffered countless sleepless nights and distressing bouts of anxiety while we were preparing to depart for the US.

My actual life experience, however, fell significantly short of my grandfather's worries and nightmares. In fact for the most part, the opposite was true. And this was reconfirmed with my biracial children, who grew up challenged but uncompromised by racism (more about this in the epilogue).

From my earliest days in the US and initial meetings with neighborhood kids and high school students, most people I met were overwhelmingly caring, supportive, and invaluable for my emotional centering. As I noted earlier, if my grandfather had witnessed their goodness and kind hearts, I believe he would have described my all-white Eastwood friends, teachers, and so many of my classmates who voted for me as their class officer as a collection of walking saints and angels. As the only minority and immigrant family from Japan in the community, we were treated with decency, kindness, and generosity. Even though we struggled with our difficult stepfather and coped with academic challenges, my peers persuaded me to believe that my life was precious and worthy as I began to emulate and learn American ways.

My grandfather would have never imagined that I could meet such good people during my high school days (e.g., Tom, Mike, and Pearl) and undergraduate years (e.g., Phil, Emil, and Stan) who would become my lifetime friends (now for over 50 years). He couldn't have known that so many key people would step up to support me as I enrolled in graduate and doctoral programs at the University of Pittsburgh and when I was hired as an assistant professor. This kind of support and kindness continued throughout my professional career. Such blessings also helped our children to grow to be successful young adults.

There were only a few individuals that I encountered throughout my life who seemed to suffer from one of the lowest human traits: A false sense of superiority over others. Nearly all the people with whom I met and interacted exhibited a sense of decency and humanistic ideals, rather than arrogance, bigotry, or intolerance of my nationality and limited ability to speak and write in the English language. Together they contributed to my ever-evolving progress towards reaching and maintaining harmony.

I firmly believe that the reason why so many people treated me with goodwill was because I practiced my grandfather's Words of Understanding. In essence its nurturing spirit was being reflected back to me by others. Therefore, I am immensely grateful to my grandfather for guiding me through his words and deeds onto the right pathways throughout my life. The honorable, dignified, and virtuous blessings he bestowed upon us were his keys into Heaven.

Chapter 15

EPILOGUE: OUR HOMELIFE, CHILDREN, FRIENDS, PARENTS, AND RETIREMENT

O<small>N THE HOME</small> front, Kathy and I experienced continual happiness as a married couple. We progressed and grew together and met our life goals together, one of which was to obtain a comfortable home. Right after our wedding we moved into a second floor, two-bedroom apartment in Wilkinsburg (about 10 miles East of downtown Pittsburgh) with a super reasonable rent of $95 per month including all utilities.

The apartment was in a three-story yellow brick building built during the 1940s with large windows on the north and east sides of the unit. Even with such reasonable rent, the rooms were relatively large with tall ceilings and a relaxed ambiance. However, because the building was standing at the corner of two hillside streets with traffic lights, the unit was relatively noisy, especially when a bus or truck stopped and passed by. After several months, however, we got used to the traffic noise and hardly noticed it.

Our first apartment (1974)

Within two years, in 1976, we were able to save $10,000 for a down payment on a two-bedroom townhouse in Robinson Township (about 15 miles west of the University of Pittsburgh and about 15 minutes from the Greater Pittsburgh International Airport). This complex had a great family-owned Italian restaurant, a large recreational facility including a party/reception room, an Olympic size swimming pool, laundry, dry cleaning services, and parking shelters. During the three years that we lived at the townhouse complex, its real estate value kept ascending. So after three years, we were able to accrue $30,000 for a down payment toward our first three-bedroom, newly-built house on a lot with an ample number of trees in the backyard. We were intently engaged in the design of the house with the builder (i.e., modification of original architectural plan, including adding a back porch with a roof and sliding glass doors, a cathedral ceiling with an open-concept living room, burnt-red and white brick outside walls instead of gray aluminum siding, etc.).

To save on building costs, I stipulated to the builder that we would do all the landscaping (i.e., lawn preparing and seeding, planting shrubberies and trees, installing railroad ties and bricks for walkway steps, etc.), which amounted to nearly $7,000 in savings. My grandfather would have been proud that I did most of the work, with Kathy's help. I purchased a Honda rototiller, 12-inch chainsaw, 10-pound sledgehammer, an assortment of shovels and mattocks, and a wheelbarrow. I also rented a trencher for installing PVC pipes underground for an automatic lawn and shrubbery watering system. I purchased several books and studied how to install a lawn and an automatic watering system.

I also learned the correct ways to plant shrubberies and trees (like my grandfather who continually took care of his flower garden). Such tasks required so much time, taking away from our weekends and holidays. But working together with Kathy was rewarding, especially when the ultimate outcome was so satisfying. The mixture of Kentucky bluegrass with tall fescue seeds thrived, and an assortment of shrubbery produced colorful flowers during spring and summer seasons.

Our first house

All our efforts paid off when we sold our house ten years later. Within one week of a real estate sales alert, three buyers outbid each other and two potential buyers lined up as back-up, giving us the down payment needed to build our current and final home.

We intensely participated again in designing and monitoring every part of the building process. Again, I took charge of all the landscaping work and other minor tasks such as wrapping the in-house plumbing pipes with tube insulation, plugging small holes with silicone glue, vacuuming floors every day for workers coming in the next day, etc. I also decided to add several flower gardens with an automatic watering system for each and individual flowerpots.

Latest house built

Custom designed and built gazebo with glass roof

A few years later I custom designed and, with my local friend Jeff's help, built a gazebo with an impact-proof plate glass roof specifically cut to size with all cedar wood framing. I wanted the gazebo to be a work of art and uniquely styled. As it was being built, I often envisioned resting in the gazebo with sake and cold beer with my grandfather as we gazed at the delightful sunset. However, as my grandfather's notes pointed out, personal effort is where most rewards rested, quite like my glass roof gazebo. Designing and building the gazebo, with an infinite number of variables to be sorted and prioritized, was far more joyful to me than finishing it. After it was completed, I felt settled, but all the intense feelings of pleasure started to dissipate.

Our daughters

In 1984 our first daughter was born. We named her Toshiko (Tosh). She instantly changed our life—besides the overwhelming joy we felt, having a child takes a lot out of you. Lack of sleep, the weariness stemming from needing to constantly attend to her, and having to spend every moment considering her needs first, It was a struggle. All parents know about this. Six years later, our second daughter, Tamiko (Tami), was born. Like most parents dealing with the birth of their second child, it's somewhat easier to know how to care for them than the first. She slept and ate well and remained healthy.

Tosh, Kathy, Tami, and me

As they grew up, we were determined to expand their horizons by exposing them to many different experiences (e.g., gymnastics, dance, piano, swimming lessons, horseback riding, playing T-ball, soccer, softball, basketball, bike riding, art workshops, Japanese story books, the arts, and culture). All these activities seemed to help them grow to be happy and healthy individuals. Since Kathy's master's degree specialization was child development, I simply supported and listened to her guidance. Her knowledge about the topic informed the values we brought to parenting, such as frequently showing and sharing an appreciation for life, providing positive encouragement (instead of continually criticizing), discussing the differences between good vs. bad manners, the importance of goal-oriented planning and practice, and spiritual intuition.

We rarely discussed the possibility that they may directly experience racism. We simply believed that an academically astute, athletically competitive, affable, healthy, and balanced child that was introspectively centered could minimize and fend off possible negative comments by their peers about their bi-racial background. However, I remained mindful of such a possibility, and, if that ensued, I was determined to bluntly address the problem immediately with kids' parents and others involved, ready with a stout direct hit to nip it in the bud.

We also decided that they should attend private Catholic schools to further reduce and effectively manage such possible liabilities. After my op-ed was published by the Pittsburgh Post-Gazette (in 1994) on teaching kids about race and gender bias, it was apparently read by several key church administrators. Our head priest requested that I serve as a board member of their Catholic grade school. This was a role my grandfather had during my grade school days. My involvement as a board member may have further reinforced the culture of the school (i.e., administrators and teachers) to remain sensitive to the concepts of equality and impartiality for all students.

We taught them lessons that corresponded with my grandfather's principles (e.g., respect of self and others, reasons for thankfulness, values of honesty and knowledge building, rewards associated with spiritual introspection and personal effort, and importance of volunteering to help others). However, even with the same parental teachings, our daughters grew up as unique individuals.

Tosh

From a young age, Tosh showed poise. She was assertive. She was someone who knew what she wanted, thought of ways to get it and got it (e.g., her favorite books to be read by mom, toys to be brought home by me, snacks she liked, and even what clothes to wear to church). From a young age, Tosh showed an aptitude for art. Her drawings were impressively creative illustrations of objects with interesting uses of color and an impressionistic style all her own. Below are photos that show her artistic talent at age six and later work at age 19.

Tosh's art at age 6 of the Cathedral of Learning (University of Pittsburgh) and at 19 of an Asian landscape

Tosh also grew-up demonstrating that she was unafraid of rolling up her sleeves and working hard to get what she wanted. As a young student, she was already ambitious, focused, and resilient. She worked hard to be better in just about all academic subjects and athletics.

As she grew into adolescence, Tosh continued to mature, becoming logical, practical, and methodical in her approach to life. She is the best in the family at saving money, mainly because of her focused determination and discipline. As a good listener and critical thinker, she is great at debating ideas with others. She can be impatient with others whom she views as shortsighted or illogical.

This combination of traits led to her being selected as a starter on the Holy Trinity Middle School's basketball team. She also earned the much-coveted annual Best Athlete Scholar of The Year award for achieving the highest-grade point average (GPA) among her coach-nominated "best" athletic peers that year. She was also a starter on the JV basketball team at Canavan High school. Later she quit because of her discomfort with the coach's treatment of the players. That coach eventually ended up resigning because of pressure from the athletes' parents and school officials.

As the older sister, Tosh was always looking out for Tami. And Tami responded well to her older sister's determination to be the best at all things she chose to do, and her caring attitude towards people in need. Yes, they sometimes fought like "cats and dogs," but they always settled down and were adoring sisters who were committed to being good to each other.

Tosh and Tami (1994)

During Tosh's senior year, Harvard University called us and asked if their admissions recruiter could interview Tosh at our house. Apparently, he read about her SAT scores in an article in the local newspaper, and he might have been an alumnus of her high school who attended Harvard. The recruiter came on a Saturday morning, and tried to convince Tosh and us that she should consider Harvard. Unfortunately, Tosh had already chosen pharmacy as her career choice, and despite having a highly ranked medical school, Harvard did not have a school of pharmacy.

After graduating high school with the third highest GPA among a class of over 100 students, Tosh enrolled into the University of Pittsburgh's Graduate School of Pharmacy

(7th ranked in the nation), and in 2008, she graduated cum laude with a Doctorate in Pharmacy.

Also, while in the doctoral program, she took up kick-boxing. This not only taught her how to defend herself from attackers but also how to make the first move to disable potential attackers. She learned that women generally cannot wait until an attacker makes the first move. She also loved Yoga and continued her participation for about a year or so. Then she enrolled in a training program that awarded her a Yoga instructor certification in 2010.

As a young woman, she increasingly became progressive and shamelessly rebellious. Her future mission, before having her children, was to dedicate her life to helping make the world a better place through excellent healthcare. She has remained inquisitive, thrives on absorbing new knowledge, and strives to continually be well informed.

Immediately after completing her doctoral program, she enrolled in a joint master's degree program with a full scholarship reserved for academically exceptional candidates (not based on need) and earned an MBA and

Master of Public and International Affairs (MPIA) degrees. With these degrees she was able to pursue her interest in global health and development.

During the summer of 2009, she traveled to Honduras with a team of doctors from the University of Pittsburgh Medical Center to provide health care services to needy rural individuals. They traveled across the country on four-wheel drive vehicles accompanied and protected by government security men who were equipped with machine guns in front of them and behind them. She also visited other developing countries such as Cuba, Trinidad, Haiti, South Africa, and Mexico to observe their healthcare systems and visualize ideas to improve the healthcare there. Her international focus is on a hold for now because she is married to an ophthalmologist and she has two young sons (Benjamin 1year old) and Samuel (3 years old), and she is expecting a third, at the time of writing.

Tosh, Sam and our grandchildren (Summer of 2022)

When Samuel was born Tosh and her husband honored me by making his middle name my first name. He's a very special grandchild who I can't wait to watch grow-up and enrich everyone's life in our family. Correspondingly, Benjamin's middle name is Mas, after my brother, who is also elated that Tosh and Sam are honoring him as a special and worthy individual.

Tami

As a young child, Tami was spontaneous, playful, and adorably erratic. She was driven by an insatiable curiosity. She was intellectually inquisitive, constantly juggling a variety of passions, hobbies, likes, and dislikes.

Tami pursued music interests during her middle school years and successfully became a baritone sax player as part of a jazz group organized by the Afro American Music Institute of Pittsburgh (AAMIP). I introduced her to the baritone sax by showing her samples of its unique sound on several jazz and rock music CDs. She liked it. So I bought her a baritone sax and I encouraged her to join AAMIP to learn how to play. She was the only non-African American student, as well as the only female in the group, but the other members really liked her musical talent. They practiced on weeknights and Saturdays and performed publicly on Sundays. She kept expanding her musical interests and learned to play a full set of drums and the Yamaha 61 keyboard workstation.

She also played basketball as a first stringer during her middle and high school years. During her junior and senior years, she joined the Amateur Athletic Union (AAU) traveling basketball team called the PA Elites (ranked as top ten teams in Pennsylvania) that played six months of the year in various cities. She was a star offensive player scoring more than 1,000 points each season.

Tami playing AAU basketball here

Tami's specialty was outside shooting. In several close games her team won by setting up a drive to the inside paint and then bullet-passing the ball back to her for a last second 3-point shot. Using this strategy, the PA Elites won games against top teams from Chicago, Cleveland, and Salem, Virginia.

Tami has always been a quick-witted social butterfly that can talk to anyone about anything. As an undergraduate student at the

University of Pittsburgh, she walked directly up to our Chancellor at a football game and introduced herself. She continued to talk with him for what seemed like 10 minutes.

She must have made quite an impression on him. Every time I ran into the Chancellor on campus he always asked, "How is Tami doing? Tell her I said hello." An accompanying faculty friend who heard him was amazed. "He knows your daughter's name? I've been here for 20 years, and he still doesn't know my name." That's because you have to know Tami, she is a social, enterprising, and extraverted warrior. She's bold and ambitious. She loves to bask in the spotlight and celebrate life.

Tami also tends to be a spontaneous young woman with a healthy joie de vivre who prefers living in the moment. She often ridicules some of her own past experiences but is always optimistic about the future. She enjoys sharing her ideas about future deeds, like taking a fantastic vacation in the Caribbean Sea, becoming a CEO, and purchasing an expensive car, such as a Tesla Model X.

At the University of Pittsburgh, Tami was elected as class president of the School of Pharmacy's doctoral program for three consecutive years until her graduation.

Tami as class president addressing faculty and students

As class president, she successfully led students on valuable school enhancement projects such as improving the School of Pharmacy's curriculum, increasing scholarship amounts to needy students through further enhanced alumni fundraising strategies, selecting unique nationally known speakers for lecture series, etc.

She also stood out as a caring individual. The Pittsburgh Post-Gazette published an article in 2008 about her success at organizing a program for convicted mothers and their children at Allegheny County Jail. It allowed convicted mothers and their children to play together away from jail facilities such as at picnics in Shadyside Park, visits to museums, afternoon movies, etc., to help maintain and nurture the bond between them. Due to the huge success and media coverage of her program in the Pittsburgh Post-Gazette at the time, she was bestowed with a Gold Award from the Girl Scouts of the United States of America for her humanitarian service to needy children and mothers.

Upon graduation she accepted a pharmacy position at Walgreens. Soon afterwards she was featured in their corporate magazine for her exceptional service to a customer who wrote to the CEO asking him to recognize Tami for saving his life. After the corporate article was published, she was so overjoyed when he brought his wife to thank her in-person at her work place where she was the head pharmacist.

Currently, she is working as a developer of specialty pharmacy programs in various locations. She travels extensively to negotiate with local hospital administrators and doctors to connect to their specialty pharmacy. The earning potential for specialty pharmacy programs is staggering—the annual revenue of over $200 million with a staff size of 15 or so is considered typical. Just this month, the CEO of the company selected Tami to lead the development of a statewide specialty pharmacy system in Hawaii—vicariously, I'm seeing my younger days from when I passed on the offer from the University of Hawaii.

My grandfather would have been proud to see our healthy and radiant girls who tackle life with gusto and have achieved academic, social, and career success with an eye to bettering the world. He may very well agree that they well-reflect their heritage of effort-driven quests and practices. Watching them grow up and achieve their goals has enhanced

Kathy's and my sense of enlightenment and feelings of gratitude.

Maintaining friendships

As my grandfather emphasized, another important note was to maintain and nurture good friendships. Thus, I kept in contact and frequently got together with my college friends Phil, Emil, Stan, and their wives and children. Fortunately, they all got along very well. We had the right ingredients for a close friendship—trust and similar values including the importance of compassion, honesty, appreciation for knowledge, and looking for and having fun. We shared many experiences going back to our fraternity days from the late 1960s to the early 1970s. Despite living several states apart (Phil in New York, Emil in New Jersey, Stan in Ohio), we have met a minimum of twice a year. It took us between 6 to 10 hours to get to Phil and his wife Sue's home, which is where we met most often.

The major reason we have chosen Phil and Sue's house to meet is because of its ideal location. Phil and Sue live in Old Forge, NY. From the southwest corner of the park at Old Forge, wide channels connect five large lakes. We can canoe from Old Forge and follow a string of lakes, ponds, rivers, and portages nearly 100 miles. The Adirondack Park that surrounds Old Forge is filled with vast forests and rolling farmlands, towns and villages, mountains and valleys, and free-flowing rivers that encompass one-third of the total land area of New York State.

It was a no-brainer to congregate at Phil and Sue's Home. During the summer seasons we rented a pontoon boat, which we filled with an assortment of beverages and appetizers and boated from lake to lake. As we traveled through colorful scenery, we swam, shared jokes, stories, and we dined at lakeside restaurants. They lived alongside a river where they docked their canoes and a small fishing boat. Tami and Tosh loved to canoe through the rivers and stop at an island to share a picnic lunch. We got together with all our friends' entire families. I was relieved and happy that Tosh and Tami enjoyed being with my friends.

During winter get-togethers, we would go skiing at nearby McCauley Mountain and go snowmobile riding on the big frozen lakes. We would ride the snowmobiles around 85 MPH on the frozen lake with the bright moon and stars enjoying your daring adventure. By age 13, Tami earned her snowmobile driving license in Old Forge. She loved cruising along the many snowmobile trails through beautiful forests and nearby lakes.

My friends Emil, me, Phil and Stan at a lake

My grandfather was right, there is nothing better than being blessed with close, good friends. Together they make me feel that I am a special and worthy person. Thus, our friendship has been one of the best protections against the hazards of life and a salient prescription for a desirable and harmonious life. After a few glasses of beer, we often shout to each other, "I love you guys! Life is Good!"

Emil's recent email highlights the tone of our close friendship. I sent an email about my worsening left eye and here is Emil's response:

"Hide, aging presents new challenges daily. However, life is always, as you know, amazingly good. We may regrettably lose our sight but our vision, always seeing the beauty in life and our families and friends, will remain crystal clear. We are blessed by our relationship, our uniqueness and our solidarity. . . . The musketeers got nothing on us. Life without friends such as you all would be much less full than it is now."

Right after Stan's passing due to his cancer, Thea (his wife) asked me to select a musical selection that reflected Stan's personality. So I sent her five special songs. Here is her email in response to my selection:

"Dear Hide,

I can't thank you enough for the energy you have put into this selection of music in honor of Stan. While I cried through the first playing of this playlist, I suspect as time goes by it will be part of my spiritual uplifting. You have captured the seasons of his life and in the final moments of Selection 5 the emotional drama of the last minutes of his life and his passing.

You have given our family a gift to be cherished. Emily has compiled it into a playlist on our Spotify and sent it to Justin and Julia. She titled it Love from Hide to Stan. Thank you.

You continue to amaze me with your thoughtfulness, intelligence, and insightfulness. Thank you for uplifting us by sharing."

Phil still calls me about four to five times per week just to check if everything is OK. Or just to leave me a message like, "Pitt's football team is dominating the Clemson Tigers! Pitt just scored with a 35-yard pass, wow!" Or simply leaving a two second message: "Hey, Hide what's up!" It may be nothing much, but every message is filled with a tone of joy that made me feel great.

Enjoying the fire pit with a few glasses of wine, he often uttered: "Hide, you are my best friend!" I often responded, "Thanks, Phil, you are the Man!"

As my grandfather noted, a close association with good friends magnifies our joy, and defuses sadness. I work to maintain and nurture close bonds. I continue to share events of our life and new developments. This focused effort over the past 50 years definitely helped keep us on the path of enlightenment.

Taking care of my aging parents

After well over 30 years of residing in Las Vegas, my aging parents (both 83 at the time) started to show signs that they needed care and assistance. My mother sent an alarming letter saying that their auto accidents were becoming frequent. Plus they were kicked out of their apartments twice in the past two years. Bill was also in trouble for not paying his doctor's bills, and my mother reported having health issues including frequent chest pain. Thus, I spent several days in Las Vegas and convinced them to move back to Pittsburgh near us. Since they rented their furnished apartment, they had very little to take back to Pittsburgh. But I still needed to handle moving tasks such as USPS postal changes, alerting the Social Security Administration, handling Bill's banking details for his pension, and arranging transport of their banged-up, 10-year-old Toyota Corolla. Such tasks, however, were easily completed within a few days.

Because I could not imagine having my stepfather live with us, we bought a small three-bedroom house about four miles from our home. This would keep them settled in one place and allow us to care for them in their final years. I also saw the advantage of not risking being evicted by the apartment owners, as they had to move several times in Las Vegas.

Photo of my parents' house

Since childhood watching my grandfather, I had learned to become a handyman, so with my local friend Jeff, I furnished and renovated my parents' house for their comfort and convenience. For example, we converted a bedroom next to their master bedroom to be a new laundry and ironing room so my mother wouldn't have to carry loads of clothes up and down the steps from the basement. We cut through a back brick wall and installed a French door to allow access to the newly added, covered porch in the back of the house so they could have their coffee and meals outside on pleasant days. I bought furniture for all the rooms and a washer and dryer. I installed a whole house fan, added a new dishwasher, and converted their electric cooking stove to gas because my mother hated cooking with electricity. Finally, I planted 40 or so gold Ahuja Forever Goldie Arborvitae evergreens around the property lines with an automatic watering system that would provide more privacy and enjoyment of their golden beauty.

When I showed my parents the house, my mother broke down in tears. She said, "We never lived in such a nice place—thank you, thank you, and thank you."

Bill smiled and simply said, "How much did this cost you?"

Because they needed monitoring, I visited their home every day. I often invited them to dinner and took them out to buffet restaurants every Sunday after church. One day my mother mentioned that she always looked forward to Sundays because she never dreamed that we could afford to go to a nice restaurant on a regular basis.

Five years after settling into their house, Bill suddenly suffered a stroke and died three days later in the hospital. He was almost 88 years old. My stepfather's funeral consisted of a special church session, in which I didn't have any sense of joy or sadness. My major feeling was relief that my mother would finally be free from his heavy-handed dictates.

Bill fell short of being an admirable and dignified individual (some may describe him as an arrogant, heartless, and abusive swindler). I was fortunate that he was not my primary role model. However, as noted by my grandfather, "Your spiritual intuition (ability to see into life and realize its deeper meaning) will help you become a strong and resilient individual that allows you to gain self-awareness and understanding. So, take time to reflect on your life and understand its complexity and blessedness to help you progress towards internal harmony and coherence."

Thus, I began to understand that I owed him thanks for playing a major role in saving my mother from a life of destitution in Japan, and my appreciation that he allowed Mas and I to come to the US. If that hadn't occurred, both Mas and I would have been denied the opportunity to meet and happily spend our lives with our marvelous family and our special friends.

Although my mother seemed very sad about his sudden death, the funeral was mainly an unceremonious processing of his ashes. His remains were buried in the huge and well-kept Allegheny County Military Veterans' Cemetery by their staff members as required by their policy (family members were not allowed to bury their deceased loved ones).

As my mother started to live alone, she asked me to teach her to drive again so she could take short trips to the grocery store, bank, and doctor's offices. She worried that asking me to drive her so often was too much of a bother. I reluctantly agreed and took her for a practice drive on a Saturday afternoon near her house.

This was a huge mistake. It was such a harrowing experience that I felt like my life was surely cut short by at least two years.

She was a terribly dangerous driver. We were lucky she did not flip the car over a hillside when she tried to abruptly veer away from an on-coming bus on a two-lane road with several cars right behind us. I quickly took over the wheel and drove us home. I kept her car key so she could never drive again. Soon afterwards I sold her car and gave her the proceeds.

About 18 months after Bill's passing, I started to notice that my mother was not doing so well. For example, she forgot to shut off the gas knobs on her stove. Luckily, it was left on for only a few hours on one Saturday afternoon. She also started to neglect her usual cleaning routines for the house and her clothes. So I started to prepare her breakfast every morning before going to the University and left something for her to eat for lunch. At dinnertime Kathy and I cooked for her or drove her to our home for dinner. I kept insisting that she move in with us but she refused. She said, "I feel so free and happy here." On the weekends Kathy and I managed the cleaning duties. On Sundays we continued taking her to church and afterward to her favorite restaurant. I was determined to make her last years the best.

Mother and me

This routine went on for another six months or so until she called me saying that she felt dizzy and could not walk. She sounded scared and confused. I immediately drove to her place. I discovered that she had fainted near her bedroom door. I instantly called 911, and soon local police and an ambulance came and took her to the nearby hospital. The hospital called me the next morning and told me that I needed to return to see her without telling me why. When I arrived, the nurse told me that my mother had died overnight of a massive stroke. She directed me to her room and said, "Please feel free to take all the time you need."

Amazingly, my mother looked well. In fact, she did not look as though she had died except that her eyes were closed. She was 90 years old. I cried in the room thinking about what she had recently told me: "I know I can't get around so much anymore, but I want you to know that I am at my happiest ever. My life is so good right now. And I pray every day thanking God for you and Kathy's kindness. You are a good son, Hide."

I also thought about her divorce from my father, which left her with few options for a life in Japan. And without breaking down how she lived a difficult life and hardship away from her home country obeying her demanding American husband. Looking at her in the hospital bed I realized how strong she was to maintain her sanity despite being subjected to abuse from Bill. Even during times of misery and stress, she had no trouble showing everyone her cheerfulness. We requested a special Catholic funeral mass for her. Right after the mass, she was buried next to Bill at the Allegheny County Military Veterans' Cemetery as she had requested.

While organizing my mother's belongings, I found her beautiful shoes and I could not give them away. Instead, I had them cased in Plexiglas so I can always remember her as an extraordinary person who was always in pursuit of harmony.

Mother's shoes on plexiglass

Because she knew she could survive, she had unceasing faith that Mas and I would be OK regardless of any hardships.

Retirement

I believe that my happiness and genuine satisfaction with my career progression contributed to the joyful home life with Kathy and my children. But after working as a research professor for 40 years, it was time to begin my focus on the remaining short years of existence.

I announced my retirement in December 2020. Kindly, several faculty and staff members emailed me their generous good wishes. Here are two appreciative comments that helped to validate my 40 year commitment and efforts.

"Hi Hide,

Word of your retirement reaches me. I want to celebrate your gifts to the School, the University, the profession and to hundreds of students and colleagues. You have been an ever selfless, hard-working faculty member who put the School and the students ahead of self. I think of the endless hours of dragging the faculty through accreditation processes and strategic plans, doctoral students through dissertations, and much more.

I think I am one who can speak with first-hand knowledge of what demands are placed upon faculty and the demands we place upon ourselves. So, it is with genuine appreciation that I salute you, your work and the retirement you have earned. You have always been extremely kind to me, a friendship not always extended to me by every faculty colleague.

The very best to you and Kathy,
Ed"

"Dear Hide,

When I became dean, then Dean Epperson told me that you would be a most loyal friend and colleague. He was absolutely correct. I was always able to count on you for support and to do what was in the best interest of the school. I was always very worried that you would retire before me. However now I am happy that you are.

You are a very good man Hide. So many of the accompaniments of the school and the Research Center were due to your leadership.

Sincerely your colleague and friend,
Larry"

I gave my focused effort to help my students, the School of Social Work, and myself. My career experience underscored that the United States, while having its imperfections, is at heart an embracing country that offers generous opportunities to those who initiate and maintain dedicated personal effort, just as my grandfather had emphasized as an important life-commitment.

In a stark contrast to grandfather's worries, my experience in the US attests to the fact that a countless number of people are receptive to being kind to others, including to racially different immigrants. Thus, I witnessed the humanity that lies inside people as consistent. With today's social and political environment in turmoil and strife, where everyone blames everyone else, I felt compelled to submit my memoir because of the benevolence that was offered to me by so many good Americans.